AFRICA
MUST BE
DEVELOPED

Agenda for the 22nd Century Domination

CHARLES MWEWA

DEDICATION

For yet to be born, sons and daughters of Africa

CONTENTS

INTRODUCTION

My dearest Dr. Munyonzwe Hamalengwa,

You and I have ruminated over Africa, its future, more than we have even chatted about the law. Imminently, law and politics are related. I remember right about the first term of the Barack Obama's presidency that you and I would sit down to a meal at your famous Greek Restaurant in Etobicoke, Ontario, Canada, and talk about the dynamic changes in US politics at the time. Here is one of the quotations from President Obama. It brought so many memories when he said this:

> To the people of poor nations, we pledge to work alongside you to make your farms flourish and let clean waters flow; to nourish starved bodies and feed hungry minds. And to those nations like ours that enjoy relative plenty, we say we can no longer afford indifference to suffering outside our borders; nor can we consume the world's resources without regard to affect. For the world has changed, and we must change with it.

Indeed, "people of poor nations" in his speech would, undoubtedly, refer to Africa and Africans. And that is what has bothered me for years. That even Obama would not find another term to describe Africa. So, as I pen this book, I am attempting to interest the reader and impress upon them my view of the future of Africa.

I believe that the term should change. *Africa must be developed.*

It should become "those nations like ours that enjoy relative plenty," because it can. Africa is a blessed continent with potential for economic growth and political distinction. But like so many Africans, I grew up believing in urban legends and myths about Africa. There have been three aspects to these, namely: Africa is cursed, poor; and underdeveloped.

I have come to the conclusion that only the last is truth. The other two are only social facts. Africa is neither cursed nor poor, though there are many countries in Africa operating far below their economic and political capacities.

Words like these, of any American president at any point in time, usually determine the attitude of the rich nations towards Africa. While they may not be taken seriously by some, Africa may peg its future on them. But whether good words about Africa would translate into foreign policy has always remained to be proven. President George W. Bush was highly rated in Africa while in the US his rating was one of the lowest of any US president before President Trump at some point. This paradox can be explained. Bush's commitment to the HIV/AIDS pandemic in Africa earned him praise among many African states.

At one of his farewell addresses in January 2009, Bush admitted that he had never been interested in Africa. His secretary of state then, Condoleezza Rice, was. Bush said that she had asked him if he would make Africa a top priority once she took over as secretary of state, and he agreed.

What am I saying? When a US president is in office, Africa is only another raw material supplier or strategic military zone and not a partner.

Talk is cheap, only Africans can develop Africa.

So, let us begin the conversation.

1 | PROBLEM DIAGONSED

July 14th, 2023, Ottawa, Canada. I arrived as usual around 10 am after having my breakfast. The table was already set, and my banner and books were exclusively displayed at the Ottawa International Book and Crafts Expo. The incident coincided with Famer's Market – so there were more people outside of the Horticultural Building along Princess Patricia Way than inside.

My next table neighbor, a fellow exhibitor, let us call her Paulina, and I exchanged greetings. Then as is usual when a White Canadian meets a Black person, they assume that, that person is from Africa.

"What part of Africa do you come from?" she asked.

"Zambia. Originally from Zambia," I answered.

I don't know how the conversation developed, but she then made a comment to the effect that Africa is a sad, struggling place. Paulina was either in the north of the sixties or south of the seventies. Either way, she looked mature and elderly.

I grinned and then responded.

"I think that Africa is just like North America."

Paulina's attention was caught. She looked at me with a somehow demeaned comportment, but smiling, nevertheless.

"But…" she began, "I thought that everyone is suffering there, and you're lucky to be in the North. Those conflicts!"

"Not all conflicts, Paulina. Just like not all the countries in the North are rich; only two thirds of the countries in North America are rich, aren't they? So is Africa – only about a third is in conflicts."

At first, Paulina seemed bedazzled. Then after a brief thought, she turned towards me and said, "You're, in fact, right. There are three countries in the North, and only Mexico is not wealthy."

"You got the point," I said.

***

Like the conversation above, the "Pauline Attitude," the problem of Africa may have been generalized and misrepresented. There is an issue there. In global parlance, reputation builds or destroys. When a continent has been reported to be barely surviving – looking like nothing meaningful is going on there, it limits its potential, at least in the sight of the world. In the end, it becomes a self-fulfilling prophecy.

Africa has problems. And so also does North America, and Europe, Asia, and other continents.

The problem of Africa is not poverty, corruption, or human rights abuses. The problem of Africa is not tribalism and lack of good leaders. The problem of Africa is not the lack of or a lame commitment to liberal democratic principles and the institutions that guarantee them.

African problems are all the above.

And these are the same problems other continents experience as well.

And the big question is: If all the other continents have similar problems as Africa, why is it that only Africa has remained marginalized and impoverished? The answer to this question is the solution to all problems that faced Africa in the past, that are facing Africa today, and that may face Africa in future.

Like Paulina, when Americans and

Europeans meet Africans, their initial reaction is that they are dealing with poor, suffering and conflicted people. And to be honest, Africans also buy into the same narrative and, eventually, begin to respond as poor, suffering and conflicted people. This behavior first only lends itself to social interactions, and before one knows it, it begins to mold the mindset, then politics and end up maiming economic potential.

Lies kill.

Every time there is war, or anarchy, or human rights violation, or national wealth misappropriations somewhere, both the people and the nation in which these are taking place slide backwards in terms of the economy and political development. For Africa, its challenge is not just to adopt and implement liberal democratic ideals in every system of government, but to empower the mind to believe that its history has not sealed its fate.

There is something very powerful in the word "liberal" that is germane to the wellbeing debate of Africa. All the connotations of liberalism – free thinking, progressiveness, moderation, and open-mindedness – are vital to Africa.

The principles of liberal democracy are

rooted in the idea of people power. People, collectively, are the masters of political power. Government itself must be the representative of the wills, wishes and aspirations of the people. Government emanates from the people. When people are not in full charge of the government, society suffers, and the government itself becomes only a tyranny of the majority.

The concept of people power lies at the very foundation of a liberal society. The test of a functional liberalism is seen in the people who vote in elections. These people should have a share of political power by determining who may rule them, and for how long. Thus, the people have the power both to appoint and remove from power those they feel deserve or do not deserve it.

This is what America and Europe did. Both emanated from barbarity and bondage and rose sharply high to embrace the idea that all are equal and deserve an equal share in governance and the economic marketplace.

Historically, when property franchises were common, the government's major role was the protection of property. As a result, the government was entrusted to those who possessed substantial properties. This happened because those with property were seen as being capable of paying most of the taxes which supported the state.

In contemporary political settings, this classical attitude to liberalism has given way to several election saboteurs. In modern political life, politicians do not discourage people from voting, even dictatorships encourage it. But in a subtle way, they may try to control the outcome of elections. This may be done through ghost voters or election rigging, etc. In either case, people are removed from the equation, leading to the destruction of the principles of liberalism.

The solution is to empower people with liberal thinking – that they control destiny, not their leaders or what other people feel and say about them. Paulina's attitude towards Africa, for example, should not form or limit Africans. Africans should aim at discovering their mental power and use it when it is feasible.

Africans must own themselves.

They should not be another race of people's property, subtly or directly. They should choose what to believe. They must consent to be governed.

The idea of the people power must translate into the consent of the governed.

This is the idea that political power does not only originate from the people, but also that the government is responsible to the people.

Government is put in place by the people on a social contract. When the government fulfills the terms of its contract, the people who put it in power may determine to keep it in power for a stipulated period of time. But when the government fails to deliver the promise, the people may choose to remove it from power through the ballot.

This is the foremost aspect of liberalism which truly empowers people to determine the direction and outcome of its government. When people are a government through their representatives, liberalism is said to be secured and popular sovereignty becomes the norm.

The Pauline Attitude is formed because Africa does seem to be in the habit of allowing some demagogues to control its thought process. So, to stand as a liberal giant, Africa must rephrase its own mantra, empower its mind to think openly, own itself as its own property, choose the leaders it wants and remove those it finds wanting in the delivery of people's goods and services, and impose its own narrative in global affairs.

Africa must think for itself.

2 | LEADERSHIP

It was around March 2003. Garth Chenda, then Executive Director of Operation Young Vote (OYV), a Non-Governmental Organization (NGO) in Zambia promoting voters' rights among the youth, had asked me to speak at the "Emerging Leaders Forum." I was very excited although I did not actually speak as I was busy making wedding preparations. But the thing that struck me the most was the word "Emerging."

I said, "Yes!"

Even then, twenty years ago, that was exactly what Africa was left with, hope in the emerging leaders that would steer their nations in prosperous directions. That emerging African leadership then is today's leaders. But sadly, what was emerging then, has continued to be a maintainer of colonial edifice, and not visionary and changers – because the problems of the last twenty years in Africa may have just tripled.

But wait a second, Africa's historical

deficiency is, in fact, its future proficiency. Africa is destined for visionary glory.

One thing that is naturally abundant to Africa is vision, just listen to political speeches across the continent. African leaders are flamboyant, tactical and overtly inventive. Someone would immediately abash that salutation, but it is the truth.

What Africa has lacked is not visionary leaders, but only sustainable visionaries. Sustainable ones have risen from time to time, only to be replaced by imposters.

The future stands poised to embrace this brand of leaders who are kin on articulating the African problem. This is a kind of leadership that has no fear of delving into new and untried ventures. It is transformational.

Unlike those who preceded it, this leadership does not want to stick to *the status quo*, which is reminiscent of the type of leaders if elected to office, they are devoid of ideas because ideas cannot come when one is in power. In other ways, the 22nd Century leadership is also transactional, and it must have been fashioned from many experiences.

National leaders, like the monarchies, are prepared outside the political arena. Leadership training is never done in a classroom. It is both a product of experience and of hard work; it is a preparation from birth. Those who aspire to be national leaders tomorrow should today demonstrate diligence in what they are doing. Leadership principles are the same; they work everywhere.

Leadership transcends academically imparted knowledge. Leadership is a calling and a vocation and is acquired through desire and responsibility. Late Dr. Myles Monroe defined responsibility as "Response-ability."

A leader responds to values that they wish to see promoted, values that work for the betterment of humanity. Leadership is influencing others towards self-sustainability and productivity.

Leadership is not the same as management. The latter is an effective and efficient way of the use of someone else's resources with the intent to give an account to the one who entrusted them with those resources. All political leaders are effectively managers of the resources of those nations to which they are accountable.

A good leader is an asset. Good leaders make good politicians, but a good politician may not make a good leader. Since leadership is universal, it entails that being a leader of any group or institution qualifies one to lead at any level of the nation. That is why wherever and whenever one leads; they should do it with the diligence that it deserves.

For Africa of the 22nd Century, the most coveted leadership kind is visionary or ethical mentorship. But why visionary? Because impromptu and maintenance leadership has failed us in the 21st Century. It has been a leadership bent on perpetuating colonial systems, only renaming some of its saliences. That leadership has constantly apron-tied Africa to Western innovation and initiative. It has not worked in Africa.

Visionary mentorship is sustainable.

Sustainable leadership is not only necessary but matters. It means planning and preparing for succession just from the day of the leader's appointment. This can only be achieved by grooming successors to continue important reforms and by keeping successful leaders a little bit longer when they are making great strides in fostering development. This is the reason why presidents with a high frequency of reshuffles are not successful. They may wake up to find they groomed no successor at all. They must reshuffle, when necessary, but always with a caveat for improvement.

One way for leaders to leave a legacy is to ensure that others share and help develop their vision. Leadership succession, therefore, means more than grooming a successor. It means distributing leadership to the various levels of the given structure so that others can carry the torch after incumbents have gone. African statesmen and women should be equipped to carry the mantle of leadership in the years to come. Preparedness should precede opportunity. It is better to be prepared without an opportunity than to have an opportunity and not be prepared.

The qualities that engender the type of visionary mentorship of the Africa of tomorrow must be all the following and more.

First, they must be charismatic. Charisma translates into passion to deliver results. To influence change, it may be necessary that leadership attracts the needed resources. Charisma is aspiration for the greatest achievement in the shortest period; it is efficiency in motion. It entails being politically savvy without sacrificing value, respect and commonsense.

Second, visionary mentors exemplify hard work. When one desires to lead a nation, they must be prepared to do so wholeheartedly, unflinching and with a dedicated attitude.

Third, African leaders who will leave a legacy are those that are hard workers. They should embrace hard work and persistence as their working philosophies. And hard work must always be among their core values. This can be achieved by setting goals and moving heaven and earth to meet them.

Fourth, a quality mentorship that will shape the future of Africa is open-mindedness. The Asian countries had moved closer to first world development in the 21st Century than even Western Europe struggled to keep its position owing to this excellence. Open-mindedness is an excellent quality that a leader of a president or prime minister should aspire for. They should pay much attention to their emotions, balancing very well with rationality and reasonableness. They should be able to question traditional values and adventure into new ways of doing things. They must be imaginative and interested in sciences, art, and beauty to enable them to perform important national as well as international functions with deliberation. This, too, is necessary to keep them tender-minded.

Fifth, if there is a condition that had both won the competition in the game of social and psychological wellbeing in the 21st Century, it had been the issue of stress. Even the progenitors of Capitalism were not prepared for how rampant and difficulty the ideals of competition would bring on leadership.

African leaders should be good at stress-management and must have necessary skills to copy. Stress is a double-edged sword; a good amount of it is necessary for success, but in excess, it can be an early killer. A responsible national leader must know that they are the nation's focus. Therefore, they will be scrutinized more and blamed more. They are responsible for failure as well as for success. Forgiveness will also prevent the jeopardies of stress.

In presidential leadership literature, it has been routine to over-praise the first African leaders who led it into independence and castigate their successors. Critical review may show that each era had its own challenges. Africa has had both credible and wimpy presidents and heads of state. This happens to all nations. Some leaders are similarly over-rated, such as the fearless Kwame Nkrumah or Nelson Mandela. Indeed, their time demanded such resoluteness, and to some point, they delivered.

However, their successors had inherited insurmountable challenges post-independence. And for Africa, it did not seem to matter whether a leader had remained in power beyond their tenure, or they only ruled for a short period of time, their record in office did not change the economic or social trajectory of their nations.

Equatorial Guinea President Teodoro Obiang Nguema Mbasogo came to power in August 1979 through a coup, accordingly, the longest-serving leader in Africa. Christopher Elnathan Okoro Cole was only African president for two days when he handed in power in 1971 in Sierra Leone.

What is, however, evident is that even in those countries with regular and free and fair electoral change of governments, there had not been a sustained number of economic results. The richest countries in Africa include some of the most ardent dictatorships as well as successful liberal democracies: Seychelles, Mauritius, Libya, South Africa, Gabon, Botswana, Equatorial Guinea, Namibia, Algeria, and Eswatini.

In Africa, dictatorship is not an economic quagmire, it is a moral question. It had seen some of the most hated dictators who had advocated more for the true liberation of Africa from colonial undercurrents than the most democratic. Robert Mugabe is still vilified in political discourse, and yet when considered in totality, he spoke more of the general wellbeing of Africa than many of the so-called African democrats did. As indicated, in Africa, neither democracy nor dictatorship has been a factor for economic emancipation, but colonialism might just be.

The elephant in the room has always been minimizing the aforementioned, especially by Western commentators, because it discredits their predictions and literature. The current crop of African leaders is a generation of a spent-up fighting force. They inherited systems totally foreign to the African tradition and have been forced to make it work on their land. The result has been fruitlessness and underdevelopment.

Africa does not just have the resources but also the brains to manage its national interests. One of the reasons why past efforts have failed to bear fruit is because African governments have been maneuvered into adopting theories that are repellant to the African system. Africans abroad are proving that they have the capacity to initiate development given all the right conditions.

However, the future of Africa will largely lie in the deconstruction of the conditions that led them here. Colonialism, slavery, and Western corporatism had been Africa's worst nightmares. These three upheavals did millennial damage to Africa unimaginable in world history.

It may surprise others that Africa has roughly been 65 years old independent on average. Colonialism existed for more than 150 years and slavery for over 400. Western corporate interests still run the economic and industrial *agenda* of Africa.

Even smart African commentators and writers fail to understand this quagmire. They read and quote Western-authored reports and literature which they quote in their dissertations, mostly supervised by Western university professors. When the write from the African perspective, they lack that originality and individuality for fear that their works would be accepted in universities. So, they regurgitate the same Western-rigged views that the problem of Africa is because of its incompetent leaders.

Western *modus operandi* in Africa has not changed. It has always been an indirect rule –

whether it was under colonialism or under corporatism. It formulates a thought, usually through media and literature and then entice African scholars to embrace it, no matter how tasteless it might sound. Take for example the views expressed in this book. It would take just one Western scholar to dismiss it as unsubstantiated and all African researchers will begin to sing the same song unverified. Moreover, Europe and America, in principle, colonized Africa by enacting a law at Berlin in 1885 without any African representation. That accursed doctrine of *terra nullius* was weaponized to seize Africa remotely and then walk on its land as if it was unoccupied.

Africa can lead itself just as Europe, America or Asia have. Leading itself does not mean that Africa should be an island. Globalization has made trade a global and regional business. But what it means is that Africa can determine its own economic and political destiny without Western interference or patronage. The 22nd Century calls for tenacious and bold African leadership that can manage the African enormous but scarce resources. The West and East must, at best, be viable trade partners and competitors.

3 | BURDEN

Milton, Ontario, Canada, 2015. I attended a concerned hosted in honor of the African Children Choir. It was delightful to hear the choir's leader stand up and announce that, "We did not come here to ask for adoptions; we have a continent to return to, to develop." To me, that was a sign that Africa had finally woken up – to believe that Africa was its own territory to develop. In the past, Africans, under the stupor of colonial haze, still believed that they were incapable of managing their own affairs.

Africans are hard workers, and African governments are not lifeless. And yet, however hard work and industry they put in, the African scale just seem not to balance. For a long time, I have pondered on this tantalizingly enigmatic scenario, and little by little I have come near to finding the answer. The answer, though, does not come that simply or uncomplicated.

Africa has been at the center of world economic survival. During slavery, Africa supplied ready but cheap manpower, and in the colonial era, raw materials for major industrialized nations. Africa has always played a key role in the world economy. Nation-states do not just cooperate; they do so at a prize. That prize is usually in the form of the balance of power. Powerful and rich nations want to dominate the world. Weak and struggling ones desire to break free from the grasp of dependency. In the end it all comes to differing national interests.

When one listens to debates or reads in the newspapers about the preoccupations of most developed nations, it all seems to center on local development. Developed nations and their governments have a local political *agenda* which they must fulfill, just like African states have theirs as well. In the US as well as in Canada, governments, however, go further than advancing home policy to catering for the poor and developing countries.

Seven percent of the US budget, for example, is said to be reserved for foreign development. This commitment is unprecedented. However, as far as the West would like to provide aid or technical support to Africa, the Western governments still have as their first obligation the development of their own local *agenda*.

Nation-states must battle their own home economies against the interests of the opposition. Failure to deliver at home in terms of the economy affects the incumbents and threatens their continuation. The balancing of state interests, domestic and foreign policy is a complex process. And this is normally reflected in the institutions of the world economy.

Thus, there can never be total submergence into the economic activities of another nation by a foreign entity even if good faith is the premise. This is not to downplay the efforts by some multinationals in their attempt to help struggling economies.

Africa cannot blindly hope that its challenges will be alleviated by activities in the international community. International communities are equally absorbed in their own challenges at home. The powerful as well as the weak do wrestle with national debts and deficits in their own countries. Even the richest nation on earth, the US, faced an insurmountable federal budget deficit of $1.4 trillion in 2023.

Africa cannot depend solely on the goodwill of the West to survive. The US is the case in point; it, too, is struggling with external and internal debt. Africa in the next century must be the lender and not the borrower. Globalization in the 21st Century failed to benefit Africa. While movements of goods and services, money and people, and ideas had been relatively easy, it seems that all move in one direction only. There is more money and resources leaving Africa to develop the West than the West is infusing money and resources in Africa. The job of the next level of African leadership is to stop this trend so that such money and resources should remain in Africa to develop Africa.

The challenge that faced Africa in the 21st Century was that foreign investment did not strike a balance between genuine international capital infusion and the right to deny bogus investors from sabotaging African resources.

When President JF Kennedy sanctioned international aid for development to Africa early in the 1960s, his vision was to see Africa achieve a level of economic development like that enjoyed by the West. In the words of Kennedy there was no good reason why in one world others should be living well while others should be suffering. Aid, therefore, was to be used as a way of equitable distribution of global resources to all.

Kennedy's belief was in good faith.

But ever since the Marshal Plan, special interests in the West have dominated the supply of aid to Africa, with huge gains. Aid is no longer a free and genuine assistance for struggling nations, but a business venture, the profits of which go to benefit few individuals who make a fortune out of the misfortune of others.

This practice has pre-empted the original notion of development, causing some people to completely disregard it as a by-word. Africa needs an economic push.

In past literature I wrote that the West held the answer for Africa. I reasoned that if the Western governments could change the way they distributed aid and insisted on having it reach the people who needed it most, Africa could make significant economic progress and save many African lives.

I was wrong.

After spending twenty years in the West, my mind was opened. I saw for myself what had always been hidden and traded in secrecy. The Western *agenda* for Africa is far from Kennedy's conception. Rhetoric seems to support a robust injection of aid resources in Africa to end poverty, but poverty is the goal.

If Africa ceases to be poor, the West will become poor. That's a rude truth to ponder. In recent trade and industrial and economic strategies, the West and Western industries are finding it unmanageable to produce basic products in the West due to production costs. The result has been outsourcing of cheap labor and abundant manpower available in China, India, and Africa.

This trend does not seem to have an end. Technology giants like Apple, Microsoft and Google are producing goods and cheap services in these areas. Even customer service is being imported from Central and South America. In US and Canada, farmers rely on temporary migrant laborers to cultivate their robust farmlands.

The West is reaching its limits. It is plateauing in terms of development. Indeed, the West has developed, and can go no further. Africa, on the other hand, can only develop further. There is no other option, whether Africa wants it or not, it must be developed, and it will.

The West is not the answer for Africa. Africa is the answer for the West.

Returning to the issue of aid, some African voices like Dambisa Moyo have eloquently lamented the disgraceful nature of Western aid to Africa. It has done nothing but impoverish Africa. In some instances, the same hand that has given out, has also taken it away. This is the case when the Western governments give aid to Africa and then demand that such aid be spent in a certain manner with their watch. Because aid attracts a handsome tax-free rebate, the same Western governments may return their monies when they appoint Western technocrats and labor to service the aid.

For example, some Western governments may donate a certain amount of aid to Africa for infrastructure development. If they then hire their own experts to be design engineers and offer several services, a large chunk of aid, through tax, will remain in their country. Africa, the supposed recipient, will receive only a small part of it. But if the aid was given as a loan, the African government involved would have to pay back the whole amount to the Western nation with interest.

This scenario has sometimes created mistrust between African governments and the bilateral nations. But more than that, the situation has caused even more miseries in Africa. For it follows quite naturally that special interests crop in and sulk all the necessary monies that were supposed to help infrastructure development and investment.

African states have resorted to multinational and international corporations for assistance. In the past four and a half decades, most aid to Africa has come in the form of concessionary loans from the International Monetary Fund (IMF) and the World Bank.

IMF was created in 1944, and its sister organization, the General Agreement on Tariffs and Trade (GATT) came in 1947. GATT was eventually replaced by the World Trade Organization (WTO) in 1995. Generally, states desire to pursue independent domestic economic policies. At the same time, these same states want to benefit from an open international economy. The role of the IMF and the WTO is to balance these two ambitious goals. In doing so, IMF and WTO not only avoid interwar protectionism, but also contribute to the avoidance of the economic doldrums which could potentially harm the whole world.

However, the two organizations, IMF and World Bank, have lent mostly to African struggling nations who are already down and cannot repay their loans even if such loans may be interest free. There is always a mantra that has been Africa's greatest demerit and the banks' greatest boost. The phrase "poverty reduction" is attached to such loans giving the impression that the banks are ending the scourge in Africa. However, critical review shows that these loans exacerbate poverty.

If I became president of say, Zambia, wouldn't I be forced to receive IMF loans? Of course, I would if my country was still poor. These IMF loans would be more sustainable in the short-term than the ones provided by private banks and bilateral partners. But long-term, my country will become poorer than before the loans were provided. Most governments in Africa are condemned to this stricture.

A lender is always more powerful than a borrower.

No student is greater than her teacher, too. A borrower is always a slave to the lender. In international relations, lending is so much a prerogative of domination as it is a catalyst of imperial advancement. In capitalistic terms, lending is a planned operation of economics, and aid is its instrument.

Aid is never free.

The World Bank, formerly the International Bank for Reconstruction and Development, was formed to assist in post-World War II recovery. But, as everyone now knows, it has since become the primary source of international aid to developing states, Africa being the quintessential hub of the developing world.

Interest defines demand, and pressure preempts decisive action. African governments are bombarded with insurmountable conflict of interest and pressure. On one hand, they must cooperate with the rest of the world in the world economy. On the other, they must meet the developmental needs of their own nations.

In theory, the developed capitalists favor free economy, even China has embraced this so far. They tend to allow the free movement of goods, services, and capital. But is it always so? Especially in the agricultural sector, exceptions loom large. Here they prefer strong domestic protectionism. The developed world can easily play the free-market economic game to its rules because they do have enough institutions and a culture to sustain it. But as we saw in the 2008-2009 bailouts and the 2020

Covid-19 pandemic, free-market has its own limits.

At present, Africa lacks both.

The global capitalistic free-market favors the West. The principles are Western based and the leaders who manage these funds and aids are Western . This is the case for the IMF and the World Bank, at least.

Having attained independence rather so recently, most African states lack the machinery to participate fully in the world economy. In fact, they have risks to contend with. And this fear is founded. Because when they have privatized their economies or asked for aid, African governments have tended to lose authority to foreign actors.

Moreover, if the current trends are to predict the future, foreign investments in Africa have not benefited African states. Foreign investment brings paradoxical sentiments. Others might even deem it an oxymoron. It is, as it were, bittersweet. Foreign capital can undoubtedly aid development. But it brings enormous challenges in foreign loan repayment. The practice has been that, due to the enormity of this foreign debt, African governments have been pressured to follow certain economic policies preconditioned on them. And to be fair, most of these policies have helped the affluent in Africa get richer. But overall, the majority of the poor Africans have not, sadly, benefited from these conditional policies.

These conditions are subtle at best. The IMF, for example, does not directly control how the nation uses its loans, but the loan must be tied to poverty reduction policies. The problem has always been that each successive African government might claim that the previous aid was mismanaged by the previous regime. So, the IMF would always claim that the "new" government has "qualified" for another loan.

Granted. The IMF exercises tremendous risk to lend to a nation that has defaulted several times on its loans. This risk is legitimate because the Fund is based on member nations' quotas. However, this seemingly ultraistic venture ends up impoverishing the African nations. Because it prevents developmental projects and infrastructure commencements. The governments that receive the pecks usually lack the political will to pay back past owed and defaulted payments. So, the debt piles up and becomes unsustainable. Future generations suffer.

The burden of Africa is a domestic crisis. Those who lend foreign investments to Africa demand that African governments repay their loans at an acceptable cost. The result has been a complicated but inescapable dilemma. In order to reassure foreign lenders that their money is safe, African governments have resorted to cutting development spending. When development spending is cut, the result is exactly the precarious situation African economies are in right now.

In addition, African governments have been forced to cut on subsidies and spending on public services and infrastructure. This has resulted in the economic colonization of Africa.

From the Scramble of Africa in the later part of the 19th Century to the end of the 1960s, Africa was incapacitated politically. Self-governance was not possible as most colonial regimes made decisions for Africa telescopically. Africans could not rise to a functional level of leadership. Its land and labor were put to service at the profit of its colonial masters. Mineral resources, power and energy went to develop the British Empire and Africa was only used as source of ready and cheap raw materials.

While most African states had attained political independence by the 1960s, to the exception of Zimbabwe which got its in 1980 and South Sudan in 2009, self-determination did not translate into economic emancipation. Africa was still tied in some form to its former colonial governments.

A new form of domination had emerged, it was economic domination. Africa needed its former masters for trade and investment. It had to abdicate its will and sometimes its rights. Africa had to play by the rules set for it. These rules or conditions have not made Africa truly free. More than then, Africa is still apron-tied to its former colonial economies.

Breaking free from economic domination by Western interests will catapult Africa as a giant economy into the 22nd Century. Africa has enough resources to sustain itself.

Already the future of Africa is beaming bright. Africa has two functioning monetary unions. These are the CFA franc zone and the Common Monetary Area (CMA). The Eco has been proposed as a common currency for the Economic Community of West African States (ECOWAS). And talks have advanced in the creation of a BRICS currency (BRICS stand for Brazil, Russia, India, China and South

Africa). The African based currencies have generally been successful in providing low inflation.

The Africa of the 22nd Century will put maximum priority on the production sector. When we speak of national poverty, we are talking about lack of productivity, on one hand, and a raging disparity in the distribution of national wealth, on the other. And when we refer to the poverty-line, we mean inadequate vehicles for the distribution of wealth. Distribution is tied to consumption. The 'haves' consume more while the 'have-nots' consume less.

The major economic stay of the developed world is the manufacturing sector. Even India and China are becoming powers due to advanced manufacturing industries, making them with the developed world, big competitors in the world economy.

The story of Africa is different. Existing patterns of relations have left Africa far behind others in building modern manufacturing capacity and locking it thereby into a subordinate position which translates into continuing to function as a source of raw materials or low-value commodities supplier.

In the 22nd Century, Africa must aspire to be not only be a source of raw materials but a producer of finished high-value commodities. To do this, Africa may have to reinvent its manufacturing potential and empower local entrepreneurs in the private sectors to actively participate in economic activities.

When governments import more than they export, they are bound to face heavy deficits that could run for years on end. This is an economic principle that does not respect whether one nation is rich or poor, developed or developing.

This is not an African problem alone.

Any nation that consumes more than it produces is in danger of serious economic troubles. Africa has been a continent of consumers. Africa consumes everything from hi-tech electronics to fashion to ideas, and even to culture.

It seemed like the Africa of the 21st Century had ceased to believe in its own prowess. African universities are still filled with books written by Western authors, its homes are filled with foreign technology, and its people take pride in obsolete ideas. If Africa is going to compete equitably in the global and regional economy in the 22nd Century, it must believe in the ingenuity of its own people.

And it will.

Africans must sacrifice comfort for diligence, a begging-mentality for industry, and political rubble rousing for risk-taking. Every nation that believes in its people survives. Africa's hope is in its people. Even with limited resources, Africa can choose to go the way of innovation and empower its people to produce what they consume and export the extra.

***

I return to the issue of economic boosting and democratization. The history of the world is the history of resolving conflicts. All the schools of political and economic thought agree that the economy is one of the most important instruments of transforming a nation into a habitat of freedom, democracy, and human rights enhancement.

Although China is under a communist regime, it, however, embraces a free-market economy which seems to be the hallmark of liberal democracy. In the 1960s, most African nations acquired political independence. They became sovereign states, and by the Westphalia model, they became entitled to personalized national image under international law.

Since the end of the Cold War, most countries embraced liberal democracy. Africa stands a better chance to gain from the ideals of liberal democracy with its emphasis on personal freedom and equality of rights, consent of the governed and free-market economy.

The challenge remains if Africa can attain this standard with a struggling economy. The other nuance to factor in is whether liberal democracy as defined and applied in the West has functioned in Africa. When it comes to Africa, the West's measure of democracy in Africa is usually tied to the holding of "free" and "fair" elections.

So, the developed world and the multinational corporations have always insisted on Africa to democratize (in the Western sense) as a precondition for further aid. As mentioned before, this insistence brings bitter sweetness. Democratizing and economic development are related reciprocally – each cause and is caused by the other. Thus, to insist on democratizing against a backdrop of poverty, debt, and a mentality of business as usual, in the 21st Century, had defeated the intention and destroyed the foundation on which aid was premised.

As I mentioned in Chapter 2, some of the richest nations in Africa have had dictatorial regimes for decades, and some of the so-called democratic nations have been poor for decades. For Africa, democracy has not translated into economic prosperity for every nation that has adopted it. It, therefore, remains for each country to determine its own type of political model it must embrace. The criteria must be economic and the protection of human rights. If a political model adopted enhances economic prosperity and protects the human rights of the people, that model has worked, no matter what it may be called.

A good example is Rwanda under Paul Kagame. The country has had a steady economic growth for the life of Kagame in power. His government invested enormous resources into soft and hard infrastructure to attract foreign direct investment (FDI). Kagame has a revolutionary political style that most commentators may categorize as dictatorial. He has been accused of restricting serious political opposition, independent media, and civil society. However, Rwandans have tolerated all that because they have seen him as a revolutionary with his people's economic wellbeing at heart. Since Rwanda is a sovereign state and Rwandans have the right to choose whom they want in power, it should be said that Rwanda is a success story under Kagame.

It is equally important to highlight that Kagame has succeeded with his local ideology in Africa where the West's economic models have failed. Rwanda provides a very powerful argument on the relationship between democracy and economic success. Under Kagame, the style of political regime chosen, in principle dictatorial, has resulted in economic growth for Rwanda.

A similar analogy may be leveled in relation to Russia. When Russia declared war on Ukraine in February 2023, the West threatened that the Russian economy would falter. By July 2023, Russia was still strong economically. The ravages of war will, inevitably, cost Russia enormously. However, if objectivity is the criteria, Russia had survived, and Ukraine was being devastated despite massive Western support.

Moreover, China has proven that ideology alone does not negate economic impact;

preconditions do and have done so for Africa. Cuts in developmental potential in order to repay loans have adversely affected African economies. If Africa is to truly democratize, the West and developed nations must rethink their democratic model as it applies to Africa. Africans themselves must rethink whether democracy has been a blessing or a curse in Africa.

In discourses of this nature, readers, commentators, and politicians usually throw away the baby with the water. When people read about the inadequacy of democracy, they may wrongly construe the discourse as advocating for demagoguism or dictatorship. Western democracy is not the only method of government available. There are various other methods which have not even been tried. The fear of not attempting the better or equally as good as democracy models, may have contributed to Africa's state of poverty.

Democracy or not, how can a nation measure its economic strength? A nation's strength is measured by the strength of its economy. In simplistic terms, the economy refers to all the means that ensure the production and use of goods and services that satisfy human wants. There are currently two measures of a nation's economic wealth: the Gross Domestic Product (GDP) and the individual well-being of the citizens. The GDP is the total market value of all goods and services produced in a country in a year. Rich nations have higher GDPs than poor ones. From year to year the GDPs of the countries of the world are compared, and these comparisons provide a measure of some economic success.

The production of goods and services ensures a country's standard of living. While productivity is not the only condition that will revamp the struggling African economies, it is a factor. As productivity begins to grow, so does the people's average income.

While a worker is an important aspect of productivity, government policy should be drafted to augment a worker's efforts. Policy should focus on providing the best of the education available so that the nation's labor force is well qualified and competent. African governments should strive to make available the tools necessary to producing goods and services which will enable them to produce things that other people will be willing to pay for.

This has been, partly, the strength of a market economy. Government policy should help boost productivity by ensuring that the workforce has access to the best possible technology.

A second measure of a nation's wealth is the well-being of its individual citizens. While GDP figures are helpful in judging the overall growth of an economy, such figures by themselves tell little about the economic worth of the citizens. The single most important measure of individual well-being is the level of income. And this is directly related to employment generation.

To see whether individuals are well taken care of, simply look at the unemployment rate. For most African states in the 21st Century, the unemployment rates had staggered. This trend should be reversed in the Africa of the 22nd Century.

A good life in terms of individual well-being will generally lead to home-ownership, property ownership and a relatively acceptable level of living. When these conditions are present, people will naturally invest more for a better future.

Many 21st Century Africans lacked even the basic goods. Some had limited or no access to good healthcare, education, and life-enriching activities. These are not luxuries; they are a right every person must have. In 22nd Century Africa, every child must have readily access to the basics of life, such as good and quality healthcare, quality and accessible education and access to safe water and a clean and green environment.

African citizens should insist on living a good life just like anyone else from any part of the world. An African child in the village somewhere has just as much right to access the best that life can offer like any child in a rich and developed nation.

A nation can borrow all it can, but if it does not produce, it's only postponing trouble. I reason that is why the wealth of nations is measured in productivity terms – GDP. The key word is "product." Diversification means multiplying productivity. It means lessening dependence on only one means of production and expanding the reserves. For the emerged African leaders, the focus should be on those resources that are sustainable, such as land, technology and the people.

In 2023, after the Covid-19 pandemic, many major economies experienced heightened inflation. These rich countries included the US, Canada, UK, etc. This was not as expected of countries known for inflation like Zimbabwe, Lebanon, and Venezuela.

Inflation is a challenge.

Absence of productivity leads to economic problems. The biggest of these, of course, is inflation. Inflation, not surprisingly, is also defined in production terms as the rapid rise in prices caused by an inadequate supply of goods and services; inflation arises from a decline in the purchasing power of the money.

In simple economic terms, this means that total demand exceeds supply. Again, this is a productivity issue. It simply means that there is less than what is required. Our problem has been that instead of producing more to curb inflation, we run into borrowing more thereby compounding the problem even further.

The money we borrow comes with strings attached. What we call conditionality is nothing but a safeguard. Safeguards are necessary for business survival.

In Africa we think that we can borrow and still be free. That's a ruse. The IMF only helps countries that are facing serious financial difficulties in paying for their imports or repaying loans. Imports are goods and services we buy from outside. IMF comes in when we fail to repay the loans we get. The IMF is a fund. Countries approach the IMF, so it's not the IMF's problem.

Africa got into economic problems because it approached the IMF, and not the other way round. Therefore, the IMF cannot be blamed for the economic problems of Africa. If Africa never borrowed (or if it borrowed and invested wisely), it would not be affected in any way by the IMF conditions.

In relation to production, we are mainly talking about agriculture and manufacturing. Agriculture or farming produces raw materials which industries use to make finished products. Recognizing this, the Bretton Woods created the World Bank which provides low-cost, long-term loans to less developed countries to develop basic industries and facilities, such as roads and electric power plants. So far, the World Bank has fulfilled its obligation and should be commended. The onus is on affected governments to channel the loans to their intended productive projects.

Production leads to export spurts. In balance of trade terms, the more we export the better. Exporting more goods and services and decreasing imports has explained why despite having constant deficit in its current account, the US continues to be the richest nation on earth. When a country buys more goods and services made abroad than it sells to foreigners that country will have balance of payment deficit. A country cannot continue to buy more than it sells indefinitely.

The future of Africa is bright, but it can be derailed by two factors, growth in population and a repeat of the 21st Century policies. Africa should impose itself on world affairs in terms of commerce and international trade. The road may not be smoother, the perils may rage, but Africa should use determination and consistency to win the day. Africa cannot cancel out its history (for all nations and continents have their own as well), but it can endeavor to rewrite it.

The mistakes of the past can be transformed into future ideas. But this will not be done by a mentality of fear, failure, and insubordination. The age of being at the receiving end should come to an end. The Africa of the 22nd Century must be a leader and should lend to other continents.

4 | CHALLENGE OF DISEASES

March 20th, 2020. I was in California with my family. We went there for vacation at Disney World. We arrived around 3 pm and immediately settled at our hotel, which was about 30 kilometers away from the world's most famous playgrounds. We could even see the towering Disney Hotel from our balcony. The kids were excited to finally enjoy all the rides and consummate the vacation pleasure.

The next day, at breakfast, we received news that Canada would be closing its borders due to the outbreak of a new disease called Covid-19. This would cut short our vacation, and the kids were not happy.

We had to go back to Canada, but how? That was the question – there was no planes flying back to Canada. Fortunately, United Airlines offered to take us back to Ontario, and by March 22nd, 2020, we landed at Pearson International Airport in Toronto.

The atmosphere was somber as it was gloomy. Our limousine driver told us that we were among the few he had picked up from the airport that day. That was the beginning of the most tumultuous series of events the Global North had experienced since 1933.

What followed were regulated closures of businesses, lockdowns, and cancellations of air travel. Death became a regular occurrence; morgues were full, and funerals ended as people feared to contract the deadly disease. Masking became a culture and later almost every living human being on earth got vaccinated.

The West were in a quandary; the very socialistic principles of bailouts they had pontificated against for years, became their panacea. And the West's Achilles' Heel was exposed: Hitherto, the West had not succumbed to an outbreak of lethal nature as Covid-19. Its national financial reserves were tested, its immune system wiped and its weakness in terms of healthcare and eldercare infrastructures decapitated.

For the sixth time in world history (see Fig.1), health war was brought right to the West's doorsteps. It was no longer a war of attrition, guerrilla warfare or space war it had dominated thus far. Guns and weapons became irrelevant, so was technology. People were dying in droves, and death was the first and last news item on all TV and radio stations.

The West were introduced to the vagaries of misery, what Africa had become accustomed to for years. Health is an economic factor, and disease is its veneer. What was true of Covid-19 in the West is what it has been in Africa with the HIV/AIDS pandemic.

WORST PANDEMICS IN THE WORLD		
Year	Pandemic	Fatalities
2019	SARS-CoV-2 (Covid-19)	6,952,522
2009	H1N1 (swine flu)	575,400
1981	HIV/AIDS	40 million
1968	H3N2 (flu A pandemic)	1 million
1957	H2N2 (Asian flu)	1.1 million
1918	H1N1 (Spanish flu)	50 million
1348/1665	Black Death (Bubonic plague)	68,596

Fig.1

I was 21 years old in 1996, a university student in Zambia, Africa, at the height of the HIV/AIDS pandemic. The pandemic had broken out more than a decade before. The impact on people's health, the economy and freedom were totally catastrophic. Forty million people died worldwide, only second from the H1N1 which broke out in 1918 and claimed fifty million people worldwide, see Fig.1.

The disease was spreading with lethal force – leaving families miserable, bread winners killed, and the governments' inefficiencies exposed.

The AIDS pandemic in Africa had reached levels where it could be considered an economic challenge. In its 2008 budget, the Zambian Government had allocated a pinchpenny to the health sector budget. It became a real challenge facing the productivity sector of the nation because it tended to shorten the lives of citizens of a productive age. The deadly disease was now not only a moral issue; it also called for serious attention and urgent economic measures.

If attitudes alone could kill, then in Africa more millions had died from attitude alone than from the scourge of HIV/AIDS. The attitude towards the pandemic in Africa had blown the health infrastructure to lethal proportions. People who showed signs of losing weight were accused of contracting the disease. Immediately one began to lose weight, they became an AIDS pariah. Many people in Africa would have lived longer with the disease had it not been for the prevailing social attitude. This was brought about, partly, due to ignorance, and, partly, due to cultural beliefs and international sentiments.

As far as the West was concerned, Africa was HIV/AIDS' headquarters. I remember in 2001 when I traveled to North America, being detained in long lines in Europe and America. Even when we had passed HIV/AIDS tests to obtain Visas, the Western systems were still suspicious of us. Therefore, all of us traveling from Africa became suspects.

Ignorance and cultural beliefs played a big role in shaping the attitudes of people towards the HIV/AIDS pandemic. There were people who thought that all who contracted the disease did so because they were promiscuous. In many African countries, like in Zambia, society looked down on all those who were believed to live loose lives. They were considered a nuisance, and therefore, deserving of contracting the disease. Many people would not look kindly at anyone who was suspected of HIV/AIDS. As a result, more sufferers died from stigmatization alone than from the disease itself.

Despite the literature on the pandemic, and the efforts by the NGOs, many people still do not understand the way the disease is contracted. To many, the people who are capable of contracting the disease are the prostitutes, the gay-lesbian communities, and those who commit adultery. Since these three types of activities, until most recently, were held to be socially and spiritually disdainful, those who are HIV positive might not be given the care they deserved. This attitude is responsible for many demises that can easily be prevented.

HIV/AIDS can be contracted in more ways than one. Although contracting it through sexual intercourse is common, it is not the only way. Innocent people can and are infected with the disease. Some people are exposed to it for no fault of theirs. This is, usually, the case with those who may be injected with unsterilized injections, or are born from infected parents, which has become manageable in recent years. Some medical accidents are also responsible for the transmission of the disease such as where blood transfusion is made without paying attention to the quality of the blood being transmitted. In many developed countries, there are now fewer or no patients dying from medical accidents as extra care is taken. There are now important medical breakthroughs in the prevention of mother-to-child transmission of the disease.

In Canada, death by deliberate infection with HIV virus is considered a crime. Someone who does not disclose of their status before engaging in sex may be sued for wrongful death by HIV. In Canada, as in many developed nations, many people who live with the disease may live with it as many as twenty years from when first diagnosed. This is partly due to the advancements in medicines and healthcare, and partly due to attitudes. People here believe that HIV and AIDS are just like any other sicknesses, just like cancer or tuberculosis.

In Africa, the fight against pandemics like Covid-19 and HIV/AIDS should be a priority of the government and the people. There are two reasons for this position. First, the government should invest in the education of the people so that they can withstand deadly diseases. Education through awareness is the primary weapon government has to fight the wrong attitudes that lead to stigmatization. From primary schools to universities, the government should design and make accessible materials and information about deadly pandemics. Many governments are doing so in Africa, but a political will is what may be lacking. If governments can be passionate about sensitizing people about what, how and why they contract the disease, it would go a long way in breaking the stigmas and prevent lethal diseases.

People themselves should avoid stigmatizing others with the disease. They must make behavioral decisions that lessen the contraction of such diseases.

Second and last, the government should invest in the procurement of vaccines, free HIV/AIDS medicines, and Personal Protective Equipment (PPEs) and create stockpiles way in advance. The Covid-19 pandemic revealed, under the Trump presidency, that even the US was unprepared for such an outbreak. Africa must learn from the failures of the West to take proactive steps in the protection of the health of its people.

5 | LIBERTY

Vigil must be applied to freedom in perpetuity. What the 19th through to the 21st centuries have shown is that, when a continent becomes naive, other continents may take advantage of it. That happened in Africa.

***

It was the year 2007. I was barely one and a half years old in Canada. I had just arrived from Africa. I was still reeling from an African mentality of absolute trust in human decency. I got a job as a peer tutor at college. I was assigned with three White Canadian girls to prepare materials and deliver instructions and guidelines to First Year students. I did most of the preparation and teaching in the team and we achieved the highest appraisal from the Assistant Director (AD). A girl in our team who I will call Megan, offered to be filing the weekly reports on my behalf, "because you're doing most of the talking," she said.

And I was fine with it.

Five weeks into the program, I was called to attend at the AD's office. I was delighted to attend as our team had scored the highest appraisal three times in a row and all thanks to my activism.

"Charles, unfortunately, we must let you go. You haven't been contributing to the team," the AD said.

"Ma'am, you must be mistaken," I responded.

Then she showed me our team report, and it was all Megan, and nothing mentioned my almost unilateral contributions.

To cut a long story short, the end was that I was not fired. I kept my job. What changed me is what the AD did next. She asked me to join her at the cafeteria and there, she gave me the first lesson in Westernology.

She told me that she originally came from Trinidad and Tobago and that she identified with me as an immigrant herself.

"Charles, this is not Africa," she started.

"You're naïve, you must exert your influence *here*; show it and demonstrate what you're doing. Don't let another person take credit for what you did."

That sort of illustrates relations between Africa and the West.

***

We live in a world with dynamic social conditions and increasing awareness of social and political rights. Fundamental human rights are enshrined in almost all national constitutions which recognize cardinal freedoms. However, there is no place where the question of human rights is such a key factor as in a democracy. It is only democracy, at the moment, to the larger extent, which has translated the slogans of justice, freedom, and equality into practice.

Social and political systems, democracy included, influence individual thinking and behavior. That is why in slave societies where rights are infringed there is no opportunity for free thinking. People are directly influenced by their sense of being right or wrong in society. Their behavior in one sector of society may have either grave or great effects on individuals and systems of another sector.

Citizens are both individuals and a society. As individuals, citizens are obliged to obey the laws. And as a society, co-operation and shared responsibility are essential for democracy to effectively work. Democracy as an ideology is, thus, an attempt at uniting the liberation of individuals with the idea of the common good. In this respect, therefore, democracy is also the rule of the people for their common good entrusted in the hands of the elected mandated by the electorate.

Democracy as it relates to the protection of liberties has one challenge. The problem is that in free societies a system of harmonizing the developments of each individual with the maintenance of social state in which the activities of all will contribute to the good of all others should be properly defined. The answers lie in self-governance in which individuals have been granted franchise to vote for individuals of their choice. This, thus, curbs political apathy and indifference.

Common political problems manifest themselves when those in power encroach upon the liberty of thought and expression directly and violently with an organized police force or military reinforcement whenever suggestions for important changes in economic, political, and social spheres are put forth. This is supplemented by organized propaganda using mass media as an instrument.

The people have a mandate to use their

franchise to elect representatives who value individual liberties. The people should be socially and politically conscious to get organized and exercise their weight for effective translation of constitutional provisions into practice. Politics should be made to rest on strong ethical foundations for politically inspiring people together with their ideals of a democratic society.

As Shi Ying states in *Longest Promise*, "If a ruler is corrupt and oppressive, people will suffer. If a ruler is virtuous and wise, the country and its people will prosper." In other words, virtuous and wise leaders use political power moderately.

Power is the fundamental tenet of politics, whether local, national, or international. There is a notable distinction between political power and power politics. The latter refers to the conduct of relations, especially among states, by the use of force, with no consideration made to right and justice. Since the views of justice and righteousness so often differ, what is usually to one nation a legitimate use of force often seems to another to be power politics. The recent example of Russia in the Russia War on Ukraine confirms this hypothesis. It is widely accepted that the love of power is the single most important spring of human action.

Political power, on the other hand, is the right that the people, who are in fact the masters of political power, willingly give to an elected government in order to rule the people. Politics without power is no politics at all. The love for power is one of the highest human qualities. The love for power not only sustains but also reinforces the three springs that are said to preoccupy human action, namely acquisitiveness, rivalry, and vanity. Thus, for the love of power, there has to be politics. And there is politics because of power. Politics itself is power generated and used.

Political power is power for good causes. Like electricity, power can be used for good or evil. In politics, power must be used for the good of the people. When power is abused, the people, not the leaders, suffer. To protect the people, power must be regulated and limited.

Political power is the key to the protection of fundamental liberties. The Oxford dictionary makes a distinction between liberty and freedom. Liberty is the state of being free within society from oppressive restrictions imposed by authority on one's way of life, behavior, or political views. Freedom is the power or right to act, speak, or think as one want. It is the duty of government to ensure that the rights of the people are guaranteed. Citizens must be free to exert their rights without interference or intimidation.

In Africa, especially the Africa is the 22nd Century, this also means respecting the wishes of the people during elections. When the people make a choice, it must be accepted. Election malpractice such as rigging, for example, is another form of political bondage, and should not be tolerated in the Africa of the 22nd Century. Any government that practices vote rigging infringes on both the freedom and the liberties of its people.

All human societies are politically organized. This political organization of society is what we call the state. The state is the center of political authority, which most societies have. The state exercises its authority by some institutions. These institutions are equipped with processes and procedures operated by chosen officials we call the government. Such institutions may include courts, legislatures, or law enforcement. In other words, government is the instrument of the state authorized by the people to organize society politically.

What then is the purpose of government? All political organizations have a purpose. The purpose of government is in its goals and objectives which the state must fulfill. There is, thus, a chain reaction: Society creates the state, and the state then should act to fulfill the goals of society. The people give the government power so that the government can in turn enable, empower, and execute on people's behalf so that the people can be free to exercise their rights. The government, which is an instrument of the state, should formulate policies and programs to promote the welfare of society. In short, the government's purpose is the happiness (prosperity), peace and order of society in which it has the mandate.

To do this, the government should commit the nation's resources and energies to it. That becomes a moral issue, or neo-morality or simply new morality (discussed at length in the next chapter). It is morality that is practical, targeting poverty, unemployment, profiteering, and exploitation of the poor by the rich, and leading to economic equality. Policies may be politically made, but the implementation and delivery must be morally carried out in order to benefit the people.

The state has two major roles. First, the

state or the government must prevent people from harming each other through the use of force, or if it is in business, through fraudulent activities. This role has, traditionally, necessitated the use of force to protect the community from external attack. This is also the role that justifies the government when it punishes those who commit acts of aggression or deception against others. This is the state's caretaker role.

Second and last, the state has a duty to intervene whenever necessary in order to promote freedom. In purely classical liberal sense, the state's only role was that of a night-watchman and nothing else, leaving people to determine their own destinies within society. But this "free market" approach has not cured societies from greed leading to economic disasters, such as in the US the financial crisis of 2008. This second role enables the government to make available such important services as security, health, education, and leisure to the people. This "reformed" approach to state ensures that government plays a coaching role in the affairs of the people, making sure that the weak and those who may not compete favorably are also protected from unfair practices.

Africa in the 22nd Century must embrace limited government. The people of Africa must be trusted. They are capable of defining right through thought and reason. They are no longer puppets to be taken advantage of by a single ruler who thinks that they can think for the people. Africans have matured to know right from wrong, and left alone, they can make good decisions. Africa must restrict legal force and delegate authority to competent professionals. This Africa is the model continent of the 22nd Century.

The idea of limited government in Africa will also ensure that regimes which hang on to power for long are eliminated. The likes of Robert Mugabe, Teodoro Obiang Nguema Mbasogo, Kenneth Kaunda, Paul Biya, Jose Eduardo dos Santos, Denis Sassou, Yoweri Museveni, Idriss Deby, Isaias Afwerki, and similarly situated leaders have put a black spot-on African democracy. Indeed, as argued in this book, there has not been a marked significance in economic terms between demagogue presidents and democrats. However, politically, the longevity of one leader in the office offsets the gains achieved through franchise. Long serving leaders monopolize power and slaughter progressive thought and divergent opinions. They rule the country as if it was a personal to holder enterprise. They portend the very worst of African statesmanship. The Africa of the 22nd Century should censure such inglorious leaders and aim for shortened tenures, as short as ten years.

As discussed in Chapter 1, longest-serving African leaders justify their longevity on state interest, such as preserving the gains of peace and order or of the economy. Thus, Kaunda of Zambia justified his 27-rule one-party government on the preservation of internal peace and order. Kagame of Rwanda justifies his dominant rule on the preservation of the economic gains.

However, as argued in this book, the solution lies in ethical mentorship – a type of leadership in which successful leaders must groom their successors from the outset. They cannot rule *ad infinitum*. For more information of ethical mentorship, one should consult my book, *Ethical Mentorship: The Missing Link in Transformational Leadership*.

***

Liberal democratic principles permit a wide

participation in political government. Many people believe that the presidential term of office should be limited to two terms only. Africa in the 21st Century lagged behind other continents in this regard. In Africa, one man may see himself as the savior of the state, leading to anarchy and lack of participation by a large majority of the citizens. This inhibits development since those who may be capable of ruling with fresh ideas are eliminated or prevented from participating.

The over-sixty-years of African allegedly freedom had been nothing but new colonial states. The colonial era has been blamed for the lack of political leadership development in Africa. During the colonial era, most people would not rise as far as a "boy" in the colonialists' homestead. Serving the "boss" was the highest job most Africans would aspire for. Those who worked for colonial "masters" in the offices were the only ones privileged to at least observe, if not dismally, how the administrative machine operated. When most colonialists left in the 1960s, Africa was left with a leadership vacuum.

However, a critical notation must be made here. This was as far as Western-type leadership was concerned. African chiefs were exceptionally competent leaders. In many Western-written literatures, when they mention "leadership" it always means Western-type of leadership. It must be stated that Western-type leadership is not a model leadership. Africans had had great leaders before the European invasion of the continent. Colonialism had mostly replaced such leaders with their own ideal. No-one should still harbor such inimical colonial thinking that Africa had no leaders of universal eloquence and capability.

In many literatures written by the West, comparison is always made to Western mode of thought. Critical review may show that Africans are better adapters than Westerners. The example of language is one in point. Although the African calligraphy and language were, mostly, translated by the Whites, they did not, however, progress beyond that standard. Africans have, comparatively and relatively, mastered all the European and American languages at far advanced rates than Whites have done. I am a good example. I have written this book (and fifty others, mostly in the English language), a language that is foreign to me, and still I can be understood. Not so many, if any, Whites, have written books in, say, Bemba or any African language.

In the 21ˢᵗ Century, Whites would have boasted of having made Africa adapt and learn its languages, etc. However, in the 22ⁿᵈ Century, Africa must rise above imitating or learning other peoples' languages and must popularize its own languages. The result will be as expected; the West will fail to compete.

Hitherto, no Western country has been able to adopt an African language in its national *lingua franca*. In the West, only English, French and Spanish – all European languages – have been adopted. There is Chinese Cantonese and Mandarin which some Western countries like Canada have tolerated, and only in business.

Many Westerners have poured scorn on accent, especially, when Africans pronounce certain Western names or words. As a law practitioner, I have appeared in more than seven tribunals in Canada. And many Canadian White adjudicators and judges have failed to pronounce my last name, *Mwewa*, correctly. But all my life, I have been made to pronounce English and Jewish names correctly. Indeed, others might argue that I have been linguistically colonized. However, there is another view. That is, thus, that, as an African, I am a better assimilator of world languages than my good White counterparts. Whites have a duty to demonstrate that they can as well learn and speak my African languages as fluently as I can speak and pronounce their Anglo-Judeo languages and names.

In a sense, Africans have been able to learn and assimilate other cultures (borrowing the French approach to colonialism). But Europe and America have not been able to totally learn the African way of life. In fact, all that Europe and America did from the inception was to erase African languages and traditions from the globe. Thus, I am called *Charles* Mwewa, instead of *Chushi* Mwewa, for example. But rarely should one find a European or American called David *Mwewa* – because, in a way, the West may construe this as Africa colonizing the West. In the 22nd Century, Africa should insist that there is an equal regard for cultural authenticity (see a comprehensive discussion on culture in Chapter 12). Africans should be ready to vanquish anything that portends historical colonialism if the West is not willing to adapt to African traditions and ways of life, names, included.

Western or European naming is *not* a sign of civilization for Africa. It is, rather, one of subjugation, historical colonialism, and, in fact, an insult. Colonialism cheated the African generations into thinking that if they spoke and articulated Western languages as the Whites did, then they were *civilized*. Thus, even in contemporary times, young Africans may be seen trying to behave and speak in Western accents as a badge of westo-centric civilization. It is not; it is a bequeathal of colonialism.

Africans who may be called by English or French names, have been *naysayers* to the African brand, and the Global North must know this, especially in the wake of the "Me-Too" and "Rights" movements. The last residue of colonialism that must be vanquished should be European-American names and associations on Black-African hegemony.

Africans try to model Western lifestyles even in politics, law, medicine, etc. More African roads are named after Western "heroes" than Western countries have named theirs after Africans.

It took nearly 150 years since Canadian confederation in 1867 for a Black person to feature on any of Canada's banknote. On December 8th, 2016, Viola Desmond became one, and, indeed, she was Black Canadian-born woman to appear on a ten-dollar banknote. By implication, any African-born Canadian may

never have no chance to be named after
something of note in Canada – and in Western
countries in general.

In reality, what, mostly, counts in the West,
is that noteworthy must be White, royal, or
Western-birth. My Canada is nobler than many
Western countries; it may be in the next two
centuries before other Western countries do
the same as Canada.

***

I now return to post-colonial African
presidents. One notable characteristic of the
post-colonial African presidents and statesmen
has been their tendency to hold on to power
longer. In Zambia, Kenneth Kaunda regarded
himself as a life-president, and so did Mobutu
Seseko of Zaire and Mugabe of Zimbabwe,
and many others. This scenario in Africa,
coupled with the undemocratic means of
ascending to power in some African nations,
had derailed the establishment of a thriving
liberal democratic tradition. And by the 1980s,
Africa was rolling backwards into what I call
the New Colonial States in which instead of
free competition in the political sphere,
succession to power was almost a family affair.

In 21ˢᵗ Century Africa, incumbents considered their presidencies as a family enterprise where they felt that they had the liberty to appoint their successors. In a purely democratic sense, the people should have the power to elect the person they want. While incumbents have a moral right to ensure that the best person succeeds them, they, however, cannot impose a candidate on the people. The case in Congo DR where Laurent Kabila was succeeded by his son, Joseph Kabila, is one example. Although Laurent Kabila was assassinated, he had not created a platform for equitable competition or for succession. All roads led to his "son" as successor. This was the one extreme. Joseph, though, at worst, through in a political quandary and pressure, capitulated and ushered in plural politics.

The other extreme is where incumbents completely annihilate any competition, even to their death, leaving total chaos. This last scenario has been responsible for disgruntlements within ruling political parties, leading to instabilities. In this scenario, the incumbent rules as a god being the epitome of law and order himself. The ruler sees all opposition to his or her rule as threats. The consequences following those who oppose him or her may range from fall from favors to even death. This was a subtle form of power holding which had crippled the Africa of the 21st Century's ability to diversify itself into a global force and compete equitably with the international community. Like the sting of a scorpion, this practice undermined progress by limiting the participating drive of the younger and open-minded generations of Africa.

This situation is very common in Africa. It is openly pursued in some countries like Zimbabwe, Sudan, Congo, and many other African nations. But it is also carried out clandestinely in other states. This usually happens in the form of election rigging or a deliberate frustration of the electoral process so that those in power, in a *defacto* move, hang on to power for an unspecified duration. Uganda's president, Yoweri Kaguta Museveni, has monopolized power this way since 1986.

In Kenya, thanks to the audacity of the Kenyan people, in 2008, the government of Mwai Kibaki would have done the same. Most people believed that Rail Odinga had won the elections. A power-sharing deal was reached later that year so as to normalize relations in the East African state.

***

There is an African new frontier emerging. If there is hope for the democratic future of Africa, it is in relation to what happened in Zambia in 2008. The election of Rupiah Banda and that of John Atta Mills in Ghana, were the quickest examples attesting to this new frontier of African politics. It is sad that Africa is behind Europe and North America in the implementation process. If Africa had done this earlier, Africa would be read from a different script altogether.

On October 30th, 2008, Zambia conducted presidential by-elections to elect a replacement for the late president, Levy Mwanawasa, who died from a hemorrhage in Paris, France, in July 2008. Before the elections, rumors began spreading that Mwanawasa had a successor in mind – his wife. But regardless, Zambians decided to honor the constitution and went to the polls to elect their fourth president, Rupiah Banda. Despite the fact that Zambia was poor and developing, it had made tremendous progress in both the election of its presidents and in the transition to power.

From 1964 when Zambia got its political independence from Britain to 1991 when

Zambia's longest serving president, Kenneth Kaunda, was defeated in an election by Frederick Chiluba, Zambia had continued on a path of democratic success. Zambia is one of the nations in Africa where elections are held every five years successfully and the people are given their constitutional right to participate in the electoral process.

A presidential election was held in Ghana on December 7th, 2008. No candidate received more than fifty percent of the votes, and so a run-off election was held on December 28th, 2008, between the two candidates who received the most votes: Nana Akufo Addo and John Atta Mills. Most foreign election monitors who covered both elections testified that they were held in an atmosphere of relative freedom and fairness. This was an antithesis to the elections held in May in Zimbabwe between Robert Mugabe and Morgan Tsvangirai. The election was close, but during a presidential run-off, the opposition leader, Tsvangirai. boycotted the election citing intimidation of his supporters by the stalwarts of the ruling ZANU-PF, the party the late Mugabe led.

What is the price of liberty in all this? One of the biggest challenges Africa faced in the

21st Century was the protection of liberties. As a fundamental tenet of liberal democracy, liberties must be safeguarded at all costs. People have inherent rights and liberties, which it is the responsibility of the governments to protect. Among these rights are the fundamental freedoms such as conscience, religion, thought, belief, opinion, and expression.

In Africa, especially the Africa of the 22nd Century, it should be the responsibility of the state to ensure that people are not only free to express their freedoms but are deliberately schooled in their civic rights and responsibilities. A free society is a breeding ground for economic alacrity and mental dexterity. In a free society, people find it easier to innovate and invent. Although in some societies where people lack certain fundamental freedoms there are notable economic advancements, it is only in liberal democratic societies where people are able to enjoy the fruit of their thought and ingenuity.

Citizens should also be allowed to exercise their democratic and political freedoms. Africa in the 21st Century had lagged behind many continents in fostering democratic and political freedoms. In many African nations, people had no right to vote for who they liked. Elections were used simply as yardstick to woo donor support. But what was even more disheartening was the fact that election results were already determined. Holding elections was a mere ruse for political engineering.

If Africa is going to emerge strong and developed in the 22nd Century, concerted effort and deliberate actions must be channeled towards the protection of people's democratic rights. Africa cannot develop economically in an environment of human rights abuses and election malpractices. There is a direct correlation between development and the protection of liberty. In societies where people know that their contributions, aspirations, and wishes will be respected, there is room for competition, innovation, and investment. This, in the final analysis, leads to economic development.

Nations which infringe on, or deny their people rights and freedoms pay a big price. And the price comes in the form of the lack of respect for the government in power, infrastructure vandalism, social irresponsibility, and election absconding. This price has all the qualities for a dysfunctional society and is a breeding ground for anarchy. This, too, justifies civil disobedience. In Apartheid South Africa, it was in order that people took it to the streets, and in some instances, vandalized national property, as a way of expressing their grievance.

Civil disobedience is justified where the government is mute to the plight of the people, especially the plight of the minority and the disenfranchised. Civil disobedience is amoral; it can deliver for the minority or the disenfranchised, and it can force a despotic government to capitulate. In South Africa, Nelson Mandela, and the African National Congress (ANC) used civil disobedience to its effectiveness. Any government that wills not to listen to reason, must be deposed through civil disobedience. However, civil disobedience must have limits. It should target only the purpose that enhances people's liberties. If civil disobedience becomes a weapon of social disturbance, it has overruled its credence.

The 21st Century problem of Africa was rooted in the abuse of power, whether that was political or military power. And the dilemma was that once a nation began on the wrong foot in terms of the protection of people's rights and freedoms, it became difficult to rectify the problem. The examples of Congo

DR and Sudan were the cases in point. When regimes disregarded the power of democratic institutions and grabbed power through guns or coups, there was created a vicious cycle of perpetual conflict and wars. The problem became even bigger because once a military regime took over the power, it refused to abdicate for fear that it would pay for its crimes and wrongs.

In Africa, especially in nations plunged by war and conflict, it is only a new and fresh-looking leader that can redeem the mistakes of the past and create a society of law and order. The answer is in the emerged African leaders. These are 22nd Century-style leaders who understand that war, conflict, and tyranny does not develop or stabilize a nation, but only disintegrate and impoverish it. Africa should insist on a modified democracy, which favors the participation of all in the governance of their countries without disregard for traditional values and practices. This so-called *New Democracy* or any name it might be assigned in future, should ensure that people determine the destiny of their own nations as a concert of consensus, cooperation and solidarity.

6 | NEO-MORALITY

The concept of morality is a universal ethic. Ethics in general seeks to investigate all aspects of human conduct, theoretical as well as practical. Ethics is primarily concerned with the basic concept of morality like *erectus* or rightness, goodness, duty, responsibility, justice, virtue, consciousness, equality, accountability, etc.

***

February 2022. I had just moved to Ottawa City, Canada's Capital, and I was in the process of acquiring a house there. To build one, I needed a job fast to qualify for mortgage as *per* the new regulations.

I got a job at the University of Ottawa's environmental law clinic. I was assigned to help on an environmental case brought by six Aboriginal youth against the Ontario Government. I met a beautiful Aboriginal youth there, call her Mano, and we quickly found ourselves chatting about the historical land grab by the Europeans and White Americans.

We had something in common.

Two months after, I attended a retreat at Whistler, a very prestigious resort in Vancouver, British Columbia.

There, I participated in a demonstrative historical enactment called "Blanket." It was presented by very astute Aboriginal influencer. Blanket illustrated how the White settlers invaded North America and methodically destroyed the First Nation's way of life and replaced it by a racist, domineering alternative.

Whites then grabbed land, impoverished the Aboriginal people and embarked on immoral and discriminatory programs. These led to residential schools, the spread of diseases among the Aboriginals and, effectively, erasing the Aboriginals' way of life.

When the presentation was over, what registered on all our faces was a word, "immorality."

What White Western colonists did to the Aboriginal people in North America was purely immoral.

"They did the same to Africa," I said, when I made a comment to the audience in response to the presentation.

And majority gathered there, mostly Whites except for me, a Black African-Canadian, and some Aboriginals, nodded their heads with tears in their eyes.

***

The relationship between morality and ethics is what an egg is to a chicken. It is believed that ethics presupposes morality which in turn presupposes freedom of the will. Ethics has progressed from people's customs and standards of behavior. Custom in the long run affects people's conscience and reason.

Ethics influence three things about us. It lays stress on our thinking capacity and accelerates developments in the field of science. It impinges on our human nature and accelerates developments in psychology. And last, ethics accelerate our developments in economics and politics by resting under our social relations.

Thus, ethics and morality affect the way we think, develop, and interact. Morality is an individual as well as a social concept. It concerns both the individual within and the society without. Moral consciousness in any field of human endeavors is an integral part of human survival.

Divorcing morality from politics is

murdering sanity from national governance. Immoral governments leave a crippled legacy in politics. Political corruption, unequal distribution of national wealth, delayed and even denied justices to the socially and economically poor of society, are among such legacies. The other is in the wide disparity between political theory (also known as political rhetoric) and actual political conditions leading to moral problems.

We have noted that morality is accelerated by the developments in various fields including science, and, thus, impinges on our thinking capabilities. Morality is imbued in reasonableness and reason itself in ethical terms is rational morality.

Morality, in its rational sense, plays a key role in today's age of science and technology. It imparts the social sense for social harmony and individual happiness. This is derived from the fact that science and technology do not happen in a vacuum. They take place in the domain of human interaction in which men and women reason. Human beings depend on each other for their development.

How then can we define morality? Morality is the scientific study of values. It is these values that enable rational human beings to interact together in social harmony. Social harmony produces an atmosphere in which men and women can freely enjoy the benefits of science and technology. Morality helps us to judge whether what we are countenancing has horrendous consequences or not. In this way, too, the proliferation of biological weaponry of mass destruction and the pollution of air and water are in a way brought under some measurable control.

Recently climate change and global warming have become moral questions. Nations must plan for the future. They must do right by bequeathing to their posterity the earth in a condition better than they found it.

The concept of morality lies at the very core of human survival. During the presidential general elections in Zambia in 2001, Nevers Mumba campaigned on the moral platform. And too many people were cynical. Many viewed this as religiosity due to the fact that Mumba's background was that of a church pastor. But what most people did not realize was that Mumba was simply trying to introduce to politics a vital aspect of moral politics.

For Africa and its challenges of corruption and undemocratic tendencies, there can never be a substitution for a politically moral leadership. The 22nd Century African leadership must understand and respect morality. They must judge what is right and implement it, and discard what is wrong and shun it.

Neo-morality is not a political ruse for winning votes, but a key and fundamental aspect of pure political maturity. It is not religious infiltration into politics, but a foundation upon which any thriving political system must be founded.

African place in global politics must be informed around its moral sense. It is a well-known fact that international politics lays little stress on morality. However, critical analysis proves that the issue is only a matter of definition. This is made so by the idiosyncratic nature of global politics. Practically, the nations of the world do know when an immoral action has been taken against them. They also know when they have taken immoral action against others, or other continents. For example, the West knows that its imposition of slavery and colonialism on Africa was wrong. Moreover, the frequency in international wars has proven this point correctly. For example, when Russia brought war against Ukraine in

2023, the world condemned it. What is an isolated action by one nation might be misunderstood by another, leading to aggression. Russia, erroneous or not, believed that it was reclaiming its former glory by invading Ukraine. Ukraine and the West, on the other hand, construed Russia's invasion as aggression.

The distinction between morality and politics is minute on matters of national sovereignty. Taking the case of land as an example, one nation believes that its people deserve enough space, and another feels that it has been denied its border line. Both nations genuinely believe that they are protecting their citizens or even defending their sovereignty. In case of an outbreak of war and its subsequent ending, many lives would have been lost on both sides. And yet each nation would claim it was in the right for its action. Again, morality is the issue. The idea of rightness, therefore, becomes the measuring rod to how serene or chaotic the world might be.

The actions of Western missionaries in Africa in the last half of the 19th Century and the first half of the 20th Century, could have been considered moral by Western formations. However, to the Africans, it meant the disruption of the African way of life, including its culture and religious orders.

Within a nation-state, morality is a key to bringing irredentism or cessions under control. For one, the scramble for Africa changed community borders and displaced tribes in Africa. In the 1960s, many countries in Africa found themselves struggling with civil wars, mostly because of displacements caused by colonialism.

Morality as a scientific study of values in international relations may be elusive but it has been enshrined in all pronouncements of recognized charters. Its usefulness, however, lies at local and national levels. Thus, dictators and dictatorships are mayhem not only to their own people but to global sanity as well. Exploitation of human beings by one another, slavery and slave trade are issues that are both moral and legal. Sub-sections (1) and (2) of Article 14 of the Constitution of Zambia, for example, regulates against slavery and forced labor.

Benignancy at local or national level entails peace and tranquility at the global level. This is enhanced by the fact that in dealing with each other, nations subscribe in practice to the ideals of what is right or wrong. Morality is a practical discipline which studies the actions of members of one society which are related to one or more foreign societies.

Morality may be political ethics, but it is the applicability of morality that gives hope to Africa. Peace and morality are related. Immoral people breed immoral actions. An innocuous leadership all over the world is the dream of its people. You least expect actions taken by immoral people to be in the interest of justice.

Corruption, discrimination, economic plunder, and many of these vices, are a product of governments or political establishments lacking a human face. The church, in partnership with the state, can unfalteringly transmit morality in its religious sense.

The church has adequate structures to not only preach morality but also channel it through into the practical aspects of human affairs. This is the reason why the controversy between church and state should not be an issue. In fact, the church and the state should join forces and partner together in the fight against corruption, for example.

Church and state cannot be said to be totally separate. The history of liberty is the history of an interwoven relationship between church and state. Until the Treaty of Westphalia in

1648, which ended the thirty-year war among the major European states, religious establishments safeguarded international relations. Despite the resolution to involve only nation-states in international dispute resolution by the Westphalia model, we have seen the reintroduction of non-state players in global politics. The church, Non-Governmental Organizations (NGOs), interest or pressure groups, to mention but a few, are necessary actors in both national and international politics.

Even in nations where the doctrine of the separation of church and state is enshrined in the constitutions, the actual practice contradicts the pronouncement. The church preaches practical morality. The state envisages the results of morality. One organ has the tools (the church) while the other (the state) has use for them. The church preaches to men and women who are a society. The state dreams of a trustworthy, industrious, and accountable society. In short, both the church and the state have the same clientele.

Where morality is effectively entrenched productivity becomes the norm and not an exception. Structurally speaking, the church must remain separate from the state, yet functionally, the two are inseparable. It is in this vein that a politician and a clergyman are both servants of the state. Moral ethics makes them both ministers in the true sense of the word.

Morality rests on the following tenets. First, it rests on accountability. Neo-morality will ensure that there is accountability in public offices for public affairs. Moral leaders are those who take responsibility for success as well as for failure. They understand that they are not the masters but custodians of public interests. They perform the duties of their jurisdiction with prudence and care knowing that they will be held accountable.

Second, neo-morality is investment-oriented. Moral leaders value the future. They don't borrow excessively so that posterity wallows in burdensome debts! For Africa, time to invest is always now because the future generation depends on what is handed over to them. Without this there can never be any economic hope. If Africa does not invest in its people, it will continue to depend on outsiders to run the economy, just the way it did in the 21st Century. This, too, will be wrong.

Third, neo-morality must foster bottom-to-top prioritization. Neo-morality is the answer to the upper-bracket-wealth-monopoly. Neo-morality demands that wealth flows from the bottom up, from the governed to the governors. Moral-conscious leaders will first meet the needs of the people before they do anything for themselves.

Fourth, neo-morality is a value-based approach. Neo-morality is a value-based ideology which seeks to inculcate honesty and integrity in its adherents. When two governments take over the power, they are on level terms. The distinction in later years will be determined by the values they attached to what was entrusted into their care. If from the outset the governments favor hard work, equality and fair distribution of national wealth, they will have less trouble in satisfying the needs of the people.

But as is often the case in many African governments, once these governments take over the power the first thing you see them doing is changing the public wardrobe, buying expensive cars, making costly and frequent trips abroad and getting flamboyant allowances on irrelevant assignments. Neo-morality demands that value precedes self-indulgence, and the people are more valuable than bureaucracies.

Fifth, neo-morality is anchored in people-centered leaders who are keen on displaying the inner quality of integrity. Integrity is both a moral and political issue. Political, because the leaders represent the people and are put in charge of a contract. The people come first before the leaders. The people are the reason why there is government, and government is, in fact, a representative of the wishes, dreams, and aspirations of the people. Integrity ensures that there is efficiency and effectiveness in the handling of public business.

Lack of integrity is detrimental to sustainable development. Leaders who lack integrity will easily steal from the national treasury and cover up their activities. They will re-channel capital into their own pockets and will not be concerned whether the people suffer or not. Men and women without integrity are plunderers and cannot be trusted to deal with other people's property. They will abuse political office for their own dubious interests.

Neo-morality is political moral ethics tailored towards the combating of poverty, unemployment, profiteering, exploitation, and economical plunder. People should demand to know the "integrity background" of their leaders before they can grant them the mandate to rule.

Sixth, neo-morality adheres to liberal democratic ideals. There is cause to respect the rights of individuals and at the same time protecting the majority. A combination of public rule and a form of government subject to restraints is a common feature of Neo-morality. Government needs to be restrained in order to preserve democracy. The presidential term of office, separation of powers, and the legal protection of the rights and freedoms of the citizens are some of the ways of protecting the people against the tyranny of the majority.

Neo-morality is consistent with the guarantee of personal freedoms, and freedoms of speech and religion, the right to private property, and the right of political opposition.

Neo-morality espouses the principle of limited government. Government is not in general charge of all society. Rather, government is an instrument serving a particular function in society. In addition, both the government and the people must abide by the same laws. No-one is above the law. And the government should ensure that it enforces the law impartially. And finally, the understanding that government emanates from the people, is responsible to them, and may be changed by them, is a basic concept of Neo-morality.

Seventh, neo-morality balances free-market thinking and a welfare state formation. Both John Locke and Adam Smith helped develop the theory of free market economy. According to this theory human needs are best served by free competition in the economic marketplace. The role of government is to enforce the rules of property and agreements that make competition possible. In doing so, the government should not direct the process.

T.H Green in the 19th Century proposed another system akin to the free market, and yet different in applicability. He believed that government should regulate liberty of contract in order to secure a higher standard of living for the less fortunate. His theory laid the foundation of the welfare state. Income tax was used as a means of redistribution of wealth; government became involved in unemployment insurance, and organized labor was encouraged.

Neo-morality is a balance between the two approaches.

For Africa, less ideology and more

pragmatism should be the norm and the approach. It is important that Africa begins to write and popularize its own models of development. Africa must wean itself from purely Western-led thinking. Because as the 21st Century has shown, such models have only led to the gross impoverishment of Africa.

7 | DIVERSITY

September 2000. Let me call her Beauty. She had just arrived from Africa a year prior and was attending her first day of First Year at a university in the City of Mississauga in Ontario Province of Canada.

A fellow student and classmate approached her. Let us call her Clementina.

Clementina was White.

"You said in class that you're from Africa?" she inquired.

"Yes," Beauty answered.

"I hear that it is an endless mass of a jungle, how do you feel having a fridge *here*?"

"We have seven fridges, five stoves and four cars in Africa. We have four farms and numerous workers," Beauty reposed.

Clementina went silent, and then said.

"Buy why is it that everything I read and hear about Africa is all poverty."

Beauty did not answer, but the two students walked a one-kilometer stretch without uttering another word.

After boarding a MiWay Mississauga Transit, Clementina smiled in Beauty's direction.

"You should tell it to the whole class – I mean, what you've just told me."

"Maybe I will," Beauty returned the smile.

Beauty is my wife.

***

Many books have been written about Africa; and a lot of talk has been given concerning Africa. Of the five continents of the world, Africa tops the list on ridicule, marginalization, and misrepresentation. Everywhere you go in the world Africa has been identified with poverty, corruption, disease, and anarchy. The international media has a stake in this. Most reports are biased, documentaries are misplaced, and the crew is foreign to the trends of Africa.

It is no fallacy that the problems of Africa are highly exaggerated. It is true that Africa is flanked by economic woos, political instabilities and health predicaments. It is true that poverty is overwhelming on the continent. It is also true that democracy is less entrenched on the third largest continent in the world. But the strategy the international media has used to document Africa's problems has created more malady than hope for the continent. While by design it is the media's responsibility to look for stories, or breaking news, where they are found, for Africa, this has not helped. It has destroyed the African image a great deal.

In international relations, just like in politics in general, perception matters. People react to you according to what they hear about you. For Africa it is not honesty reporting, it is extremely uncensored reporting. Many people know more about Africa than they do from their own local news. But they only know about Africa in a generic sense. For example, they may know that there are constant civil wars in Africa. They may not know that Africa is a large continent with 53 countries, and only about only six countries are in some form of civil war. In statistical terms, we are talking about less than twelve percent of African nations.

African governments and NGOs may be inept at disclosing their figures, including discrediting evidence, for two reasons. First, it may be unnecessary not to do so because powerful nations may already know what the reality is. The American Central Intelligence Agency (C.I.A) does compile facts and challenges of most nations on the globe. The

C.I.A and many such agencies may have more resources and techno-how than most African governments. This puts the African governments at a disadvantage in terms of what they can or cannot divulge.

But second, and if not more importantly, most of what is reported about Africa is because of the influence of special interests and lobbyists. It all comes to, as the adage goes, an elephant in the room. Even if these special interests and lobbyists know that divulging certain information about Africa may taint its image abroad, they choose to do so for-profit reasons. To them it is business as usual. If Africa is portrayed in a more progressive way, these groups fear the flow of aid and other grants will diminish.

The image of Africa is marred by irresponsible reporting. People of civilized societies have been hoodwinked and misled at worst. Those who have not travelled see Africa as a jungle of sick and miserable human beings. And this is justified by the images which greet them on television. Producers of these images seem to be good at what they do. How else can you convince someone to donate their hard-earned dollars except by appealing to their feelings? And there is no emotional inducing sight than that of a dirty-looking and hopeless child living in what in the Western society may seem unbelievable.

By writing this I am not lamping together the philanthropic and humanitarian actions of those who genuinely lobby and canvass for Africa. There are many people who are risking their lives for the African causes. The Canadian couple who almost died in Kenya is a good example. John Bergen, 70, was attacked on July 9th, 2008, by a gang of robbers armed with machetes, and he suffered broken arms and a skull fracture. His 63-year-old wife Eloise was tied up and sexually assaulted. The couple had moved from Vernon, B.C., to Kenya in March 2008 to do missionary work and run programs to feed the poor. The couple decided that they would shortly return home to Canada for healing, but sooner rather than later, go back to their work in Kenya. From whichever angle you look at it, this is an amazing story of compassion and human sacrifice.

This story is not meant to adduce that all those claiming to work for the betterment of Africa should suffer harm to prove their sincerity. It simply shows that there are people and governments and organizations that are genuinely serving the real problems most Africans are facing. Such individuals and organizations need to be commended. But for those who use the misery of Africa to advance their personal agendas and amass wealth, their efforts are a letdown for Africa. It is such people and organizations which have perpetually painted a despondent picture about Africa.

I have lived in Africa for over twenty years. I know about the African way of life in and out. But I have also been acquainted and lived in the West since 1998. I know the ways of life of the rich and developed. There are definitely some sharp contrasts in the way Africans and Westerners view life. These differences, however, dissolve as you interact with both people. You begin to realize that there are more things in common than what differentiates the two peoples. Both people are warm, lovely, and gregarious. Although by economic standards more people are empowered in the West, Africans too show varied signs of a desire to improve.

Africa is one of the most urban dwelled continents on the globe. The urban African lives boom with life and activities. There are big cities in Africa such as Cairo in Egypt, Johannesburg in the Republic of South Africa, to mention but a few. In fact, most people in African cities live relatively comfortably. In Lusaka, the Capital city of Zambia, where I have spent most of my young adult life, there are more automobiles on the roads than the available space can allow. There are a good number of people driving brand name cars like the Mercedes Benz, the BMWs, etc.

Many people in Africa own their own houses. But there is also a growing number of homeless people. The First World Nations do also have homeless people on their streets. Because of the flamboyant images they see in movies and read about in Western-authored books, most Africans think there are no poor people in the First World Nation. But this notion changes when they travel. The West as well as Africa both harbor the poor, except that the disparity between the rich and the poor is much narrower in the West.

Many young Africans dream of living in the West someday. Many people in Africa also erroneously think that the moment they will step on the Western soil their problems will automatically disappear. Some people who might have made it very big in Africa find themselves dejected once they travel. Although to a larger extent most people who live in the West are economically better placed to succeed than their counterpart in Africa, success is relative. Liberal societies offer personal freedom and the economic opportunities for all. But success is not guaranteed for everyone. Some emerge extremely wealthy such as the founder of CNN Ted Turner, the late founder of Rogers Communications Ted Rogers or the founder of Microsoft Bill Gates. But most people are in between living their lives normally.

Africa in the 22nd Century must strive to remove the economic disparity that exists between the rich and the poor. It must, in the words of President Obama, strive "to make [its] farms flourish and let clean waters flow; to nourish starved bodies and feed hungry minds." But this in way should not diminish the fact that some people in Africa are already cultivating flourishing farms, drinking clean water, taking care of their bodies, and feeding their minds. When only negativity is reported about a people, they try to live up to that standard. It is some sort of a self-fulfilling prophecy. In some ways this has been true about Africa. But Africans are exactly how they have been labeled; Africans are hardworking, creative, and peace-loving people.

The strength of Africa is its diversity. The land of Africa teems with viable natural resources. It is the land of mineral deposits. Africa is a place of gigantic rain forests, extensive grasslands, wonderful rivers and lakes and a thriving civilization. Africa is alive. And this is a reality known and deliberately kept a secret by those who plunder African resources. If there is a place of varieties, it is under the African skies. Here dwell dark people in Sudan, the dark-brown peoples of East, Central and West Africa. Blacks and whites live side by side in South Africa and North Africa is home to light-skinned Africans! All these add variety to the color code.

Africa, too, teems with languages; magnificent languages of the Bantu, the Semites, the Kushites, the Kwa, and the click sound in the languages of the inhabitants of South Africa. Here is the land of an eternal summer in which tourists from all over the world come to bask. This is the Africa that I know; the Africa in which I have lived, and the Africa rarely portrayed in motion and pictures.

Technology is booming in Africa, though not beating at the same rhythm as that of the West. However, in 22nd Century, African technology will cradle future civilizations, just as it did in pre-slavery and colonialism eras.

Africa is a house of splendid courtesy. You are not a stranger in the African milieu. The concept of a nuclear family does not suit an African environment. All are brothers. All are sisters. Africa is like a large family of variety and style.

There are problems in Africa. True. Over twenty-six countries in Africa south of the Sahara are categorized as the highly indebted poorest countries of the world. To be poor and indebted is a dangerous combination. As a people who seek to exert their dignity and humanness in world affairs, Africans must begin to refuse to be placed under this category of nations. It is not attractive, and neither is it honorable to be poor and indebted. Africans must learn that all nations of the world have problems that are peculiar to them. But they will be offended to be called poor. Poverty is the greatest evil against human sanity. Poverty is a shame. To be poor is tumultuous but to be poorest is absurdity. No one with human dignity desires to be or see his fellow human beings remain poor. It is against human nature.

However, poverty in Africa has been overtly politicized. The politicization of the African poverty problem has cost Africa more in terms of human resource development and creativity. While poverty is being used as an excuse, many philanthropic societies have benefited immensely transacting in African poverty. Some multilateral organizations need African poverty to continue to make profit.

Poverty is, thus, a two-edged sword.

Africa's status in the world has been used against it, thereby creating more conditions of perpetual poverty. Early in the 1990s, Anglo-American Corporation (AAC) in Zambia bought the Konkola Copper Mines to develop the copper mines and create employment for Zambians. After a few years these mineral giants had left the mines citing their inability to make profits. But by the time AAC left Zambia, the mines were not better than they were before. This is just one in which foreign investors take advantage of the poor. And Africa will not see her full potential if she does not empower her own people to own and run her industries.

Africa's is unique.

The African mindsets and philosophies are unique to Africa. Africans are fiscally conservative, but socially progressive. Africans believe in the principle of capitalism and value. Long before the invention of currency Africans practiced market economics through batter system, which was the exchange of goods for goods. But Africans also regarded their poor and needy. A kind of society in which people collaborated in economic and social terms was a common practice in the African setting. Family was defined broadly to include extended relations. Respect for other people's privacy and property was not just a social obligation, it was a virtue. Even in African villages today, people still cooperate in social and economic matters.

Africa can benefit immensely from her culture of cooperation. The African principle of life calls for cooperation and community-consciousness. In Africa you expect to eat even if you don't work. You expect life to be easy and to acquire things free. The African communities lived in extended families in which everyone was related. Some sort of common ownership was possible, but this was based on mutual cooperation. This is not African communism or socialism. This communal approach to life is based on values and not on ideology. This approach is a gift from birth, inherent and enshrined in their hearts.

Trust is inevitable in Africa. You can't afford not to trust someone. You respect elders and value the gift of life. Her inevitability to trust has many times led the African into trouble. Trust is a flawless human endowment. But trust has also landed Africa in problems. In the past Africa has entrusted their livelihood and their lives into the hands of foreigners.

Whether it was during colonialism when Africa unwittingly abdicated her land and resources into the colonial maters' care or during privatization when African governments have entrusted her economic resources to foreign investors, Africa has not been rewarded in the similar way. Foreign corporations amass wealth at the expense of the struggling African economies.

Africans are used as cheap labor and their governments never see the benefit of these investments. Profits accrued from Africa are invested in the investor's places of origin, leaving Africa economically worse than she was before.

Africa cannot afford to be naïve any longer. It has to adapt to changing economic and sociopolitical trends. It cannot simply think that she is fulfilling a social obligation by being courteous to strangers. When it comes to making decisions and choices that border on the economic and social wellbeing of her people, Africa must not relent but be tough and consistent.

With the coming of globalization, however, this dispensation of distraught naivety is now fading away. What is important is for both the West and Africa to recognize that they have aspects which each need. Africa needs the Western technology and expertise just like the West need the African courtesy and raw materials. Self-determination is only possible when the forces of legal and moral whims recognize the inherent capacity a people have to rule themselves. Mutual understanding and the concept on national sovereignty must be taken literally as a balancing gesture. Africans must rise to the challenge and take interest as leaders in global affairs. Only when this is successfully done, will Africa never again be a victim of marginalization.

8 | ELEPHANT IN THE ROOM

Until recently, it was believed that African people had a much lower mental caliber than their counterparts the whites. African people were thought to be devoid of any mental power to think productively or to innovate. It was strongly believed that they were an inferior race and had unsharpened intellectual abilities. The problem with these presumptions is that they lack verifiable proofs. For example, the word 'intelligence' itself has never been properly defined. For a long time, psychologists have defined intelligence only as, "That which intelligent tests measure."

To a layman this does not make sense. It is tautology. It's like saying intelligence is intelligence. However, difficult as the definition might seem, experts in the field of intelligence have come to look at intelligent people as ones who subscribe to three indices: Practical problem solving, verbal abilities and social competency.

Looking at these very critically we see that they too are problematic. What do we mean by practical problem solving? If we say that an African is dull because he can't solve mathematics or measure length, or construct a skyscraper, or produce a cure for a disease, are we being fair? An African has done all that. What if we say that an African has no verbal abilities are we saying the truth? For sure Africa has never had a Shakespeare, a Chaucer, a C.S Lewis or a Wordsworth, but Africa had great oral recitalists and highly skilled local poets and dramatists.

I am an African, and my works speak for themselves.

Africans could not have constructed their oratorical based on Cicero's rhetoric techniques, but they had great and wise speakers of all times. In addition, as mentioned elsewhere in this book, Africans have mastered all the known world languages, including English, French, Spanish and many European languages. Africans have demonstrated that they have a much nimbler language brain than credit is given.

For example, Europeans have not shown that they can speak fluently most known African languages. But Africa has. In the past, it was insinuated that Europe and America had won the day because they had managed to impose their languages upon Africans. But no-one ever reasoned that Africans are better and faster learners of languages. In fact, Africa has close to 2000 languages, and is home to approximately one-third of the world's languages, second only to Asia with about 2,300 languages. The US is third with between 350 and 430 languages, and Europe is fourth with about 200 languages. If language is a sign of intelligence, then Africa has it in abundance.

Similarly, we can't say that Africans have no social competency. Africa could even measure highly. Life in Africa is basically social. Families are extended to include first or even second cousins, nephews, and nieces. People visit each other, perform common rituals, and gather in *indabas* for deliberation. Sociolinguistically, Africans are aptly competent. Rules of greeting are highly incorporated and African languages are highly symbolic and pragmatic.

Experiments done on intelligence were unfortunately in America and Europe. For those which were done in the US, African-Americans and Hispanic, and Whites were used. One of these experiments done postulated that, "Black and Hispanic seven-year-olds perform on reading, writing, math and science tests at about the level of White or Asian 13-year-olds." This report was however hampered by historical racism and the controversy in the expression "middle class." This is often modified in the US to mean Whites, and all others belong to the lower class. With this view in mind, it becomes even more difficult to believe in such a conclusion. Putting it simply, if you take the middle-class Black, and a middle-class White, subject them to similar conditions and to unbiased testing, they would both produce superior results on intelligent testing. Western intelligence tests are notoriously biased and are mostly performed by White people.

The philosophies of both Hegel and Kant on race have been found to be mostly unknown, hidden or brutally biased against Blacks. And what is more, it is completely a waste of time and resources to even dwell on White philosophers writing about Blacks with what we already know about slavery and colonialism.

Africans are, by no means, an inferior race. As argued in Chapter 7, they are a unique race. In past discourse, I have written extensively on race issues such as the postulations of Genetic Drift and Natural Selection methodologies. I have attempted to replicate works done on oriental and other races of people. Then there was Hitler with his extermination of both Blacks and Jews because of faulty reasoning on his Aryan Prometheans of Mankind. It is historical notice how such racist thinking can lead to. Then there have been arguments about Africa being the cradle of civilization, the oldest continent. Then there has been debates whether God Himself is White or His first human creatures, Adam and Even where White, Brown, or Black. Some have gone to such lame extremes to state that the first man himself was not White (for Adam in Greek is a word *adama* which means reddish brown).

Having spent half of my life in Africa and half in America, I find such discourse misplaced and irrelevant. Day-to-day experience with people of all races and backgrounds has taught me that we are all one race, the human race, no matter our different color pigmentation.

In Canada, there has been progress in revisiting past atrocities committed by Whites against the Aboriginal peoples. White communities in Canada are showing exceptional commitment to equalize relations and where possible to apologize for the mistakes of their ancestors in the way they treated the Aboriginals and Blacks and the Chinese. There is, clearly, an understanding that the older generations that subjugated and plundered Africa for close to 500 years (including new-colonialism) were mistaken. However, the length of time it took for these historical injustices is cause for concern if Whites can truly reform and completely accept Blacks as their equals. Africa must be vigilant and never again drop its guard.

In the 22nd Century, Africa must not allow Whites to repeat what they did to Africa for close to 500 years. The past of Africa is a shameful chapter in world history. "Lest we forget," should be as much an African anthem as it was a commemoration of Queen Victoria's Diamond Jubilee, ironically, the most acquisitive of all British monarchies.

9 | HISTORY

It was in 1996 at the University of Zambia (UNZA) in a history class. The lecturer proudly introduced two textbooks, one of them was clearly written by a European academic. The so-called supplementary copy was written by Ali Al'amin Mazrui. I can't remember either of the titles.

I sat there as the dutiful lecturer substantiated the theories of the African history. I was in First Year of university, but I was not naïve. Later that day, we were given a homework assignment to do. I visited the UNZA library and to my shock, that gargantuan of a library was rustic, huge, and stocked with 99.9 percent of Western-written books. It was then that I decided to rewrite Zambian literature and change the mindset of future readers. I started with *Zambia Struggles of My People: Western Contribution to Corruption in Africa*, a magnum opus of over one thousand one hundred pages, covering history, politics, law, economics, culture, education, technology, religion, and everything in between. The subtitle itself was conveniently suggested by

Hamalengwa, then a very successful Toronto lawyer. He also suggested that I publish it in its entirety under one umbrella in line with the purpose I had disclosed to him for my penning it.

He was right.

It was Prof. Dickson Mwansa, Vice-Chancellor of the Zambian Open University (ZAOU) who later captured the spirit that wrote the book when he remarked, thus, "The combination of the two makes this book about the biggest book of our time written and focusing on Zambia. It is encyclopedic in coverage but lucidly and coherently held together. It is written with passion and concern, hence its title *Struggles of My People*."

How appropriate.

I wanted the reader to grasp the enormity of the African problem, without having to cross reference. It took me six years to pen, 500 books quoted to write one book, numerous websites and articles consulted, and over two thousand footnotes.

Some events in life are so prominent that failure to remember them is tantamount to treason. Remembering events of such nature are necessary for the following reasons. First, humans have the tendency to repeat history.

For Africa, sadly, history just cannot stop repeating itself.

Second, it helps to strengthen the determination never to undergo such experiences again. Again, sadly, as will be shown, Africa has had to experience the same events over and over.

Third, it acts as a guide and a constant reminder of how a particular group of people got where they are. This has the propensity to help them prepare to fight any encroachment that might threaten their existence and well-being.

Fourth, it acts as a warning to future perpetrators and last, it is a lesson for future generations, and this is proper.

Africa has become its history. There are three events that define Africa, no matter from what angle one contemplates looking. These are the Trans-Atlantic Slavery, colonialism, and neo-colonialism (corporate plunder). Fig.2 illustrates the three epochs.

PLUNDER OF AFRICA		
Duration	Upheaval	Impact
1526-1867	Trans-Atlantic Slavery	12.5 million people out of 86 million (15%)
1880-1975	Colonialism of Africa	US$31.17 billion GDP in 1960
19765-present	Neo-colonialism	US$40 per year leave Africa

Fig.2

The combination of the Trans-Atlantic Slave Trade, colonialism, and neo-colonialism has covered a period of close to 500 years. Within this period, there has been no gap; there has been no duration or time when White Europe and White America have ceased from plundering African resources, human and material.

In short, Europe and America are non-existent without Africa.

The Trans-Atlantic Slave Trade was not the

creation of the Africans, as history would have us believe. Some Western nations that perpetrated this evil trade deny ostensibly that Africans sold themselves and they (the slave masters) only stayed on the coast. But we should not forget that the Trans-Atlantic Slavery started with a kidnapping phase in which Africans were abducted and were taken to Europe and America as slaves.

It has been estimated that during the whole 400 years of the Trans-Atlantic Slavery, only 13 million Africans were shipped out, 11 million landed safely on the other side and two million died on the way through disease, torture or deliberately being thrown into the sea to lighten the load or for insurance purposes. In Fig.2, I have attempted to error on the side of caution and have selected the lowest possible estimates. This way, I will not misrepresent history or falsely accuse White Europe and White America of excesses.

However, despite the estimates, it has always been Whites who have plundered Africa. Black Africans have not sold or bought White slaves. Black Africans have not traveled the world in search of other races of people to plunder. Even when Black Africans have acquired residences and citizenships in Europe or America, they have been marginalized, segregated, victimized through racism, and faced disparities in work, education, and economic establishment.

These are historical facts.

Once, one of my blood brothers praised me for having "made" it in Canada. And this is what I told him, "Whites traveled far to Africa and made Africans slaves and low labor force right on the African continent. What makes you think that when I come to their shore, they would suddenly make me their boss?"

It is as true as it can be painful.

During the first 400 years of White invasion of Africa, to the slave masters, a Black African was no human, but a monkey deprived of his tail. Today, the Western media still label an African as hopeless and Africa itself as a hopeless continent. To accept such labels is tantamount to self-kill or suicide. And because Africans continue to be pessimistic about these things, today, these things are manifesting through other forms.

In 2013, Hamalengwa had represented a Black criminal suspect, an accused. I accompanied him for a trial. This client was caught on camera raping a White woman. What was so repulsing was the manner in which he conducted himself after the assault. He left her there lying unconscious in the cold, and then he had an after-thought. He retreated, spat on the poor woman, and kicked her in the side. It was as if he was saying, "Trash!"

This man was a fellow Black man. I felt sick, so sick that I could not concentrate. It was morally wrong, ethically unsanitary, and spiritually condescending. It was inhuman and tasteless.

It is immoral to kick someone when they are already down, and hopelessly vulnerable. That is exactly what Whites have done to Africa, just like my tasteless African brother did to that helpless White woman.

Wrong is wrong, no matter who does it, Black or White.

We have had crippling and subtle slavery in the past 60 years in the names of sustainable development, liberalization, structural adjustment programs (SAP), privatization, globalization, HIPC, regional integration and NEPAD, etc.

"Charles, are you mad, you are now questioning the world survival?"

You may object.

I was intrigued one day when I decided to

tune to an Amnesty International documentary on poverty and SAP in Ecuador, a Central American nation. This passionate narrator showed pathetic results of the programs initiated by IMF in that nation. A few people had 'benefited' but the majority, even the last hope they had, had gone. Then the narrator made a comment that vituperated my sense of genius.

"These programs," he began, "are theories tested on innocent lands, which will never be tried on Europe and America."

I was baffled, I hope you are.

From August 31st to September 7th, 2001, a "World Conference against Racism, Racial Discrimination, Xenophobia and Related Intolerance" was held in Durban, South Africa.

Major former slave masters failed to acknowledge that slave trade had 'killed' Africa, in fact, some even had either boycotted or walked out of the conference, especially, when the issue of reparations was raised.

Why did they refuse to pay slave reparations? The West still argue that slavery and slave trade are just an appalling tragedy of the history of humanity. They seem to advance a theory that slavery was legal at the time and, therefore, it cannot be called a crime against humanity. And then, like now there has always been justification for slavery. Slave trade and slavery, though lucrative on the part of Europe and America, left a legacy that keeps on haunting Africa, like a rebellious demon.

The first thing that slavery leaves behind is bitterness. Bitterness is not pleasant. It affects a person's mind as well as their tastes in life. A bitter person is resentful, harsh, and virulent. They rarely enjoy life. They cease to appreciate themselves. This is the primary legacy of slave trade and slavery with which Africa was left.

And Blacks are sometimes mocked for being angry and bitter – because they must be – slavery and other inhuman upheavals could have done nothing less to them.

1982 is a watershed year in Canadian history. Of course, Canada adopted a new constitution which included a *Charter of Rights and Freedoms* (the "*Charter*"). But in that year, another monumental act of civilization was enacted into law. The Canadian *Criminal Code* (the "*Code*") was amended to include what are now known as "rape shield" provisions. To encourage women to report sexual assaults, Parliament shielded the woman by outlining in Sections 276 and 277 of the *Code* that courts would not admit victim's sexual history from into evidence. Before these provisions, it was common for perpetrators, mostly men, to argue that the woman brought the rape onto herself. They argued about aspects which included prostitution, inappropriate dressing, or other surreptitious behaviors. In short, they maintained that the victim caused their own crime, basically.

And interesting, judges, who were mostly White males, acquitted them on such flippant argumentations. But in 1982, Canada did the right thing – it righted a wrong in the rape shield provisions of the *Code*.

The world, many times, treat Africa the same year rape victims used to be treated before the rape shield provisions in the *Code* in Canada. To complicate matters, most of Africans are black in color, and this has, historically, fit well into the biblical narrative that sees Satan and evil as black.

Until relatively recently, many Black Africans failed to consider themselves as finely made. They doubted their own complexion and appearance. They even bought into the sad narrative that they were an accident of nature. They might appreciate others but not themselves.

Is it little wonder that even in public media

Africa seems to ridicule its own inventions and praise anything done or made elsewhere. In Zambia, like in most African countries, most of what is programed on television is foreign. It is not so much because there is poverty that over 90 percent of what passes through their eyes every day comes from overseas. It has everything to do with a slave, dependent mentality. There is nothing which the West has that Africa does not have. The whole world is interdependent, and no one is an island.

The other effect of slavery, apart from shame, disgrace, and humiliation, is despondency. To be despondent or dejected is to be at one's lowest ebb in terms of self-esteem. One's spirit is crushed. It is a state of heart brokenness.

In real life if one's heart is said to be broken, that someone is a dead person. Metaphorically, to be heartbroken is to be in a condition of dysfunctional. It is to lose interest in progress and in life. It is to be quick to surrender or even to deny good for oneself. And this is what slavery did to Africa.

Since 1526, Africa has not existed free of European or American control. This might surprise some. Even the 60 years of the so-called African independence (which is only a fraction of the domination of Africa by Europe and America), basically 13 percent of the time since Africa was 'discovered" by the Whites, Africa has been under White rule, in some form.

In fact, Africa is more a mental slave than it is an economic slave. One of the biggest challenges that Africa faces is mental enslavement. Slavery has the propensity to deny one what truly belongs to them. Freedom is not only a virtue; it is a right as well. To be politically free and yet to remain mentally in bondage is not real freedom. If Africa does not emancipate itself mentally it will again be selling, not its human resources this time, but its birthright.

Africans should pride themselves as a people with a mental will to plan their own destiny, however costly that might be. Africa should desist from mental dependence on others and decolonize itself from prejudicial elements. The sons and daughters of the former slave traders should not be blamed for all this. Both should see each other as allies and should work hard to make up for the mistakes of their ancestors.

But caution must be exercised; whereas Africa has acknowledged making a grievous mistake in selling its people and sovereign rights in the past, now it must be careful that it doesn't sell its mind again. If slavery had deprived Africa of its inner feel and spiritual energy, colonialism (discussed later) robbed it of its economic and political will.

Africa was known as the darkest continent until such men as Dr. Livingstone, the missionary, and H.M Stanley, the traveler, started to disseminate stories about it. But this was also misinformation. Africa had seen civilization far earlier than either Europe or America. Some historians have observed that in the early 19th Century, the rest of the dark continent were in the hands of barbarous native tribes, whose frequent wars and outrageous slave raiding horrified European opinion when they were made known by early missionaries and travelers. They conclude that the pity aroused by their stories was one of the reasons why the people of Europe undertook what they regarded as civilized missions to Africa.

This hypothesis may be questionable for two reasons. First, the voyages were long and dangers. And second, it seems to give the impression that both the slave and barbaric nature of the Africans would have ended them had Europeans not trekked there.

The history of the world is one of barbarism. Even in the Bible, wars and massacres were the only reaction to aggression. People killed each other for land, food, tools and sometimes for nothing but hatred.

Africa was not the only continent which harbored the so-called barbarians. If one considers the Dark Ages, they were the age of European barbarism. Between 375 and 1066, mass movement of the barbarian Teutonic tribes took place in Western Europe. It was so severe that it affected even the church. What in an actual sense made Europe better than Africa was the Industrial Revolution.

The Revolution tended to lower the child mortality rates and improved Europe's standards of living. However, it was not the entire Europe that was experiencing a glorious age. All along, European historians painted a picture that Europe was flourishing at this time and, hence, that many acquired territories in order to develop Africa.

But at this time, with the exception of England, most countries in Europe were groping and wallowing in poverty. It has been argued that during this time most countries rushed to the New World (America) because of the discovery of gold there. This is only part of the story. For example, the great Irish Migration in 1847 to America was not because of the discovery of gold in California, but due to the Irish Potato famine in 1846.

Of course, gold was not the only reason for the enormous emigration from Europe in the second half of the 19th Century. Poverty and politics also played their part. Mass migration from Europe to America was caused even more, perhaps, by fear of starvation at home than by hope of abundance abroad.

The supposition that pity was the main reason for colonizing Africa may, therefore, be unfounded. The same reasons for European migrations to America were the same for the scrambling for Africa in the 1880s. As someone has brilliantly commented, "Pity was only an understudy to the ordinary motives for imperial expansion."

For England, it might have been the desire to expand markets for raw materials and investment in new ventures but for the rest, or the majority of the European countries, it was due to poverty, fear of starvation and looking for greener pastures.

Africa was not a dark continent to the Europeans; it was an opportunity. When missionaries and explorers and travelers started to bring news about the gold, silver, copper, vegetation, rivers, and virgin lands, it was like a bright star had suddenly appeared in heaven. Even the nature of the scramble for Africa illustrates this.

Various powers were so frequently colliding with each other that only two courses were possible. Either there would be a European war, or else the powers would have to divide Africa into sphere of influences and agree not to trespass on each other's territory. And this last option took place in Germany at the Berlin Conference in 1884-1885.

The act is deemed a robbery as there were no African representatives. European nations present at the conference declared Africa *terra nullius* or empty land. According to *Al Jazeera*, Britain acquired, or stolen Africa territories became extensions of itself. Slavery was a source of immense wealth for Britain, and fueled industries such as shipbuilding, banking, and insurance. In need of replacement sources of wealth, politicians developed the idea of "legitimate commerce," whereby African forced labor in African countries would produce resources shipped to enrich Britain.

In addition to artefacts, European powers

stole African land, palm oil, gold, ivory, diamonds, cotton, rubber, skulls, coal, etc. Even when Britain, for example, "abolished" indigenous slavery, it replaced it with slave labor. The West used discriminatory practices and policies to discourage the African local to compete favorably with the European powers.

***

Like slavery, colonialism was again the creation of the White European countries. To put it conceptually, the over-three-hundred years of taking from Africa gave birth to the direct invasion of Africa. In other words, the West was not satisfied with merely taking African able-bodied people; it decided to return to occupy Africa itself. Europeans "punitive expeditions" confiscated or looted African artefacts from the so-called tribes of savages" and stored them in Western museums. Western museums are complicit in colonialism and would not return stolen artefacts to Africa after the fact. Africa made the West. Britain would not return what it clearly grabbed from Africa to stock in museums, choosing, rather, to place them under a policy of "retain and explain." That is, Britain knows that the artefacts were looted from Africa but is unwilling to return them to Africa.

Britain and Western Europe stole Africa. This is what their museums confirm. Africans have been guardians of loveliness. A German archaeologist, Leo Frobenius, was fascinated by African creativity in artefacts that he preferred to claim that African artefacts, in fact, originated from Greece.

Whites' modus operandi has not changed when it comes to Africa. They either pay lip service or pretend to be humble and caring when with Africans but in the end, they grab whatever is revealed to them and endorse it as their own. This happens in every sphere of life – technology included.

The impression created by the world is that Africa is devoid of innovation and creativity. That Africans cannot invent anything of note. The truth is that Africans are always inventing things, but the West take credit for such.

In 1910, South Africa successfully hosted the soccer world cup. I was in Canada, and I followed how soccer commentators ran out of ideas and words, because their predictions came to naught. They had predicted that Africa would be unable to host a game of such magnitude. Then something else happened at the 2010 World Cup.

Vuvuzelas.

A Canadian commentator was beside himself when word started spreading that the vuvuzelas were invented in Africa. Although there is controverse whether it was Prophet Isiah Shembe, Neil van Schalkwyk, or Freddie "Saddam" Maake who invented it, there is a dispute that it originated in Africa. And that is where the issues began. Western commentators tried everything to discredit the vuvuzelas. To some in the West, vuvuzelas were too noisy, unhealthy or something else.

Fédération Internationale de Football Association or International Federation of Association Football or FIFA in short, banned the vuvuzelas after the 2010 World Cup allegedly because of the backlash from the "global community." By the "global community," it meant, mostly, Western countries. FIFA would not allow vuvuzelas to be used in the 2014, 2018 and 2022 World Cup tournaments.

Sports slavery and colonialism.

It was clearly because Africa showed some creativity that the West (through FIFA) banned vuvuzelas. If those were invented by a small boy in Europe or America, they would have been hailed as a work of genius. This Western attitude towards African products and inventions, has reduced Africa into a dumping ground for Western products and services. The story of African artefacts in Western museums is testament of the ingenuity of African creativity. To dominate the competition and to have a competitive advantage, the West go to some length to demean African products and services. Yet even 10 Downing Street and 1600 Pennsylvania Avenue in London and Washington, DC, respectively, could have been built by African brainpower and hands.

Al Jazeera reports, this, "In 1899, Henry Labouchère, the MP for Middlesex, described the process by which territory was acquired during a parliamentary meeting. 'Someone belonging to one company, or another meets a black man. Of course, he has an interpreter with him. He asks the black man if he is proprietor of certain land, and if he will sign a paper, he shall have a bottle of gin. The black man at once accepts; a paper is put before him, and he is told to make his mark on it, which he does. And then we say that we have made a treaty by which all the rights in that country of the emperor, king, or chief, or whatever you call him, have been given over to us. That is the origin of all these treaties.'"

I have dealt extensively about bogus treaties colonialists drew up to grab African kingdoms and lands in *Struggles of My People*. No space will be given to that topic in this book. However, it suffices to mention that for a mere bottle of beer, Western colonialists went ahead and grabbed precious land in Africa.

***

Europeans invented all sorts of stratagems to dispirit the Africans. Western imperialists and colonialists called Black Africans primitive and degenerate, feeble minded and unattractive and firewood of Hell. Missionary movements introduced racism to Africa.

Historically, the entire protestant missionary movement in Africa began from a racist base. When that great Moravian minister of the Gospel, Count Zingendorf, decided to go to Africa as a missionary in 1731, he asked King Christian VI of Denmark for permission to go and preach to the Blacks. And this was the King's remarks: "How can you do that? They are the firewood of hell! It is impossible for a black person ever to go to heaven. What a fool you are!"

This was in the same period when slave trade was flourishing. The prevailing theology then was that a Black man had no soul. And yet many times Africans are silenced that White missionaries loved the African continent and built for them hospitals and schools. Did the Whites build them, or they were built for them by the Blacks?

In January 2018, then as US president, Donald Trump referred to African countries, Haiti, and El Salvador as "shithole" nations. The same way White slavers and colonialists called Black Africans during slavery and colonialism.

***

In Chapter 2, groundwork was developed around the discredited claims that Africa is poor because of incompetent leadership. It was, in fact, colonialists who failed to empower Africans for Western-style leadership.

Christian racism was severe. One of the evils this racism did was failure to empower the Africans. Colonialists built schools and employed European teachers, built hospitals and engaged European doctors and nurses.

And later after independence, these powers came and ridiculed Africans that they had failed to rule themselves.

It was barely after 20 years of independence that the West began to claim victory in Africa, namely, that Black Africans had failed to rule their states. In fact, this narrative was so pronounced and commonplace that Africans themselves began to buy into it. Ignorant African writers would even put it into books, scolding their own governments as corrupt and inefficient.

Context is very important.

The West had controlled Africa through the slavery eras up to 350 years. Immediately after that, colonialism was imposed upon African for close to another 150 years. In the 1960s, most African states got "independence." The West "left" the first African leaders with governance structures patterned upon Western style. And yet for close to 430 years, Western colonialists, and slave masters never allowed Africans to govern, not even to be assistant commissioners. In Zambia, for example, the first crop of leaders had been mere clerks in lower government ranks. And these became presidents and ministers in government. Still,

CHARLES MWEWA

the former colonial masters expected them to
run governments efficiently, without resources
and national leadership experiences.

When the Whites colonized Africa, they did
not empower the Blacks for Western-style
leadership. African leadership is not
substandard; Western colonialists failed
African in leadership. Even now in the West,
educated Africans are subjected to managerial
positions if they are lucky, or to secondary
citizens in the Western countries in which they
are citizens. They are held to an abnormal
standard of perfection which they themselves
are unable to replicate. They are condemned to
racial injustice and promotional deficiency.
The income disparities between educated
Whites and educated Blacks in Europe and
America is huge, so huge that educated Blacks
come out like educated slaves.

Uneducated Whites run corporations and
industries in Africa. They usurp lucrative
positions and control massive African
resources just because they are Whites, and
nothing else. Slavery and colonialism dealt
such a blow to the African consciousness that
a typical African think that every White person
who comes to Africa is intelligent, competent,
and capable. African governments selectively

138

offer profitable contracts to White-dominated companies at the expense of their own people.

There is a false assumption in Africa that everything a White person touches turns into gold. The opposite is the case. Everything the Whites touched, as far as Africa was concerned, turned to ashes.

White colonialists and slavers left a legacy of bigotry in African leadership. Brother Andrew in his book *Battle for Africa* has been very quick to pin-point a particular black nationalist as saying: "This is not discrimination by bloody white settlers or colonialist against Africans, but discrimination by Africans against Africans." This is in order to justify that Africans are the architects of their own political doom. But this is also null founded. The missionaries and colonialists did not want to involve Africans in decision-making processes. They were only content to use them as 'boys' and servants. So, when these Europeans went and left power to the Africans, the new African leadership was like fish out of water. The observation Brother Andrew made earlier is the correct one: "Perhaps our greatest shortcoming in Africa has been our failure to develop leadership among native Christians." This goes the same for the settlers and missionaries as well as the colonialists. What this observation entails is that African leaders who inherited governments from their former masters were like inexperienced drivers in big automobiles. What do you expect from that, accidents, of course. That is exactly what happened to Africa.

Many African economies, let alone political governing systems, are in serious damaged conditions. As is the case when a car breaks down, it can only be fixed by the manufacturer who designed it. Africa repeatedly rushes to the former masters for aid and technocratic help.

Indeed, 60 years of the so-called African self-rule or independence cannot reverse over 150 years of colonialism. It is my hypothesis in this book that the 22nd Century will be African age – because by then Africa would have been experimenting its governance for about 150 years – exactly as much as it had been under colonial rule. By the 22nd Century, all the colonial thinking would have vanquished from its psyche.

Africa shall then be developed.

The 22nd Century will see a brand-new Africa. In some cases, the entire old colonial systems will be uprooted with the implantation of new systems. Africa will be able to run its own affairs as smoothly as the West run theirs, just as it did 500 years ago before European penetration.

Africa is the future of the world.

10 | THE COMMITMENT

In August 2019, my family vacated at the beautiful island of Hawaii. Of the places we toured, was one where President Obama grew up. It was déjà vu for me. I started to remember the speech line reproduced in Chapter 1 that President Obama made. Hawaii gave me a resolve to keep the memories of Africa alive, no matter how long I lived in the West.

In 1988, Bishop Joe Imakando and I visited a small village in Guatemala called Almolonga. We attended a world congress on prayer. At that congress, I found myself praying to God to give me a burden for Africa.

And God did.

Hawaii was a commitment to that original prayer, that I would never forget or neglect Africa. Hawaii was a revelation and a lesson. I saw how the US had honored many indigenous heroes there. Streets are named after local indigenous people. And we toured the island, it was educational to see the synergy between Western representation coming together and seamlessly fusing with indigenous symbolism.

That is how the West should do to Africa –
realizing that the West and Africa can co-exist
as equals. The West should use its unique
position to aid Africa in its quest to find a
balance in economic, political, and
international relational aspects of globalization.
If the West is going to be naïve, or to show a
lame commitment to Africa, not only will
Africa continue to be poorer, but the world
economy will suffer as well.

As the 2008-2009 economic crisis, the 2019
Covid-19 pandemic and the 2023 Russia
invasion of Ukraine have taught us, the world
is not a structure of untouchable states, but of
vulnerable states. Nations of the world are not
immune to the global crisis. Issues such as
global warming, disease, poverty, oil and
energy are concerns of all nations, rich and
poor alike.

The idea that one nation can engage another
in productivity terms only when it can benefit
from such engagement is an oxymoron. Even
if self-interest is the norm, the nations of the
world are realizing that depend on each other,
including on Africa. Nigeria, for example
produces oil, and OPEC knows that Nigeria is
crucial to the world oil sanity. Some nations in
West Africa produce coffee which Western

states imbibe. South Africa provides the world with unique reserve of gold and diamond.

Western states should not see Africa as a dumping ground for experimental drugs, technology, or products. Africa should not be viewed as source of outsourcing for cheap labor, either. Africa should be considered a partner in global trade and development. Africa has the raw materials, but this is not up for grabs, it must be traded.

People, natural and environmental resources of Africa have a capacity to save the world. When you travel from city to another in developed nations, you rarely see empty space. Land is already occupied with industries or factories. Africa still retains most of the arable land. As the world becomes more interdependent, Africa will provide the much-needed land and space to produce necessities to keep the world moving for another century.

Western policy towards Africa should be based on fair play. African leaders must insist that they are accrued a place they deserve in fundamental decisions which may have serious global consequences. It is, indeed, unbelievable that the continent of Africa with its size and history still has no permanent representation at the United Nations. Ironically, 37 percent of nations that make up the Security Council were present at the racist and colonial Berlin Congress in 1884-85. The countries present were Austria-Hungary, Belgium, Denmark, France, Germany, Great Britain, Italy, the Netherlands, Portugal, Russia, Spain, Sweden-Norway, Turkey, and the US. Those which are permanent members of the Security Council are China, France, Russia, the United Kingdom, and the US.

Africa, as it was at the Berlin Congress, has important decisions being made about it at the UN Security Council without permanent membership. Africa is still being shared by the world.

If there is anything the world is learning every day, it is that no one nation is invincible. History has proven that smaller nations have the capacity to become big and powerful. History has also shown us that powerful nations and empires collapse. Rome and Egypt were once mighty empires. A policy of equitable corporation will ensure that Africa tailors her creativity towards satisfying the demand of the West. When Africa is seen as dumping ground, it demoralizes its competence in world economic, social, and technological development. Africa should exert its resolve to compete and play fairly with other nations in the global marketplace.

Africa plays a viable strategic place in the military and power domination of some Western states. Most powerful nations know that if they are going to win over terrorism and piracy and secure a global advantage over certain non-state actors, they need Africa. For these reasons, many of these nations have secured centers, set up strategic missions and deployed their own men and women in uniform in certain places. They do this because they know that these African centers are vital to their quest to win over enemies. This model of corporation with Africa is one-sided. It is premised on the simple concept of self-interest. To such powers, Africa is only a means to the end.

Partnering with Africa must be based on a moral understanding that it is both necessary and humane to cooperate with Africa. Many developed countries are well-placed to help Africa conquer its challenges of poverty, AIDS, corruption, and bad governance brought upon it by the same powers. Many developed nations have a moral obligation to support Africa economically because, indirectly or directly, they have contributed to the state of Africa today. The West has advanced at the expense of Africa.

Globalization has made the world into a small and reachable global village. The internet and advances in communication are necessitating the sharing of information and inventions more than ever before. It now takes just a click of a computer mouse for one part of the world to know what is happening in another part. Business transactions are no longer confined to boundaries. People can conduct business across the globe at the stroke of a computer keyboard. E-commerce is opening new vistas of trade and business. There has never been a time in the history of international trade when monies move so swiftly across borders. If there was a time to involve Africa in global trade and commerce, it is now. Africa has everything to offer. Not only land and labor, but Africans everywhere are also becoming a force in the global economy. Fifty years ago, no one would have predicted that South Korea would be a force in the electronic technology. Africa, too, is rising, and in less time than the world expects, Africa will be leading the world in several respects.

Africa is not only important to the world for strategic and moral reasons. Major economic events in the world have shown that what happens in one part of the world affects the rest of the world. The oil crisis of 1973 and 1979, the international debt crisis of the 1980s, the world stock market crisis of October 1987, the Asian financial crisis of 1997 and 1998, the global financial crisis of 2008 which began in the US, and the 2019 Covid-19 pandemic, show the importance of international co-operation.

All signs point to increased economic interdependence among states. Both realists (whose emphasis on international relations is on the strategic importance of cooperation, especially when that cooperation may enhance their military and economic influence) and liberals (whose perspective on international relations emphasize mutual beneficial properties of economic and power exchanges, especially when such a relation will lead to the preservation of peace among nation states) are awaking to the reality that whatever the motive, the effect of international cooperation benefit all.

From the observations made above, it is both prudent and civil to consider Africa as a major player in international development. Whether it is poverty or issues of bad governance, whatever happens in Africa may in one way or the other affect the entire world. The issues of Africa continue to preoccupy even unwilling regimes.

Rich and developed nations help the poor and developing nations. This is vital in times of humanitarian disasters. The West and rich nations, at the moment, cannot simply watch as insurgents and rebels and terrorists devastate not only nations in which they have strategic advantages, but Africa as well. Whether it is due to Katrina in New Orleans, or Tsunami in Indonesia, or hurricanes in Burma or ethnic cleansing in Kosovo or genocides in Darfur, or FRG9 insurgency in Haiti, or 2023 Sudan conflict or, indeed, the Russia-Ukraine war, powerful nations have moral and political obligations to defend the weak and vulnerable.

In recent years, increased conflicts in Africa, especially the war in Congo DR and the genocides in Darfur, and military conflicts in Sudan, are calling upon the UN Security Council to redefine the mission of peacekeeping in Africa. If the Rwanda genocide is a symbol of the worse things to come, the UN cannot only define its mission as peacekeeping in Africa. The African Union lacks the resources and infrastructure to provide collective defence and to combat increased and sophisticated wars in Africa at the moment. It needs the full force of the UN to help it reduce wars and protect the innocent. To ensure collective security, especially when dealing with African conflicts, the UN should extend the meaning of peacekeeping to peacemaking. If this approach had been taken in 1994, over a million people would not have been massacred in Rwanda. The UN has a responsibility to protect those who are victims of human right abuses through humanitarian aid, and military intervention, if necessary.

11 | CULTURE

International politics classify nations as super-powers, big nations, and small nations. The criterion is usually military, political, and economic but not cultural. Culture is never a yardstick for measuring a nation's greatness.

The culture of a nation is the sub-total of all the beliefs and ways of life of that people. This is why it is important to guard one's culture and it is the same reason why the culture of another country cannot be better than that of the other.

Western culture cannot liberate Africa. And Western educated elites have failed to run the economies of Africa. Japan has shown that cultural integration is good but not necessary. This view is seen by some as the reason why Western education has not helped the poverty of Africa.

True.

African patriots can only be bred from Africa itself because they understand the African culture. I do not by saying this disapprove Western training for African leadership. I am one of those who received Western education, but not after graduating from an African University. What I contend is the socio-economic enslavement by the IMF and the World Bank which cannot be ended by the Western educated elites. Saving Africa should be a collective effort by the locally educated as well as the internationally educated Africans. In this way, like in Japan, we can borrow some ideas from else-where and add them to ours in order to help bring sustainable development to Africa.

The culture of Africa is one of the best blessings Africa has from God. It is neither superior nor inferior to any because cultures are not comparable. What is good in one culture should be true to others as well. Decent living, respect for human rights and dignity are accepted everywhere as tenets of a good culture.

The African culture promotes a sense of community and kinship. Such a culture is a breeding ground for sound economic principles and Africans should take advantage of that. Africa ought not to borrow a culture from elsewhere and this is what the peoples of Africa should teach to their children and their children's children. It is absurd to imitate another culture and feel you are independent. Most people who have relocated still hold on to their cultures even if they live in the West. It is bigotry that in the nineteenth century Africa's forefathers were sold as slaves and in the twenty-first century Africa should sell herself culturally.

African names, music, dressing, and traditions should be jealously kept because that is what defines an African. It is, however, not a crime to integrate various cultures for the purposes of harmonious living together. African leaders especially, have a moral obligation to test foreign theories and assumptions to check whether they agree with cardinal African cultural beliefs, especially if that can help eliminate poverty and disease.

Cultural respect is a fundamental aspect of multiculturalism. A multicultural society consists of more than one culture existing side by side. Within a multicultural society are multicultural people or individuals of different cultural backgrounds living alongside each other. They have usually reached this harmonious state of coexistence by respecting the cultural differences of each other while upholding the qualities that unite them. Often a multicultural person is one who has come from another country or cultural milieu and finds a living among other groups. This person may try to maintain his or her own culture with all its norms and systems of beliefs or may choose to integrate and acquire not only another language but another culture as well. This last aspect was such an experience Malika Oufkir found herself in. She describes in her book, La Prisonniere, how she came to learn to live in and assimilate two cultures in complete harmony despite her background. She tells of how she came to realize that her life would not be in Morocco, her native land, and the country with its history, language and customs which she deeply loved. Malika had been abused and imprisoned by the King of Morocco and upon her release from prison she swung from deepest resentment and the sincere wish to feel no more hatred for her abusers. She only came to rediscover her peace of mind and her love for Morocco in the desert. She narrates how she had travelled back and forth across it, her favorite destination being Tafilalet desert, the cradle of her paternal ancestors. The desert soothed her. It reconciled her with her past and helped her understand that she was just passing through.

She felt she came from that land, she

belonged to it body and soul. In the midst of the ochre dunes, among those vast expanses of golden sand, in the palm groves inhabited by Blue Men, she realized where her roots laid. She knew that she was "Moroccan through and through, to the core of [her] being," (Oufkir 392).

Malika immigrated to France and there she adopted a new language and culture. She was no longer only Moroccan; she had become a multicultural person. Malika says, "I have become French, through the language, culture, mentality, and intellect. The two are no longer incompatible. In me, East, and West at last cohabit in peace," (Oufkir 392).

Our world is shaped by many forces, and culture is one of those powerful forces that act on us. Culture is central to what we see, how we make sense of what we see, and how we express ourselves.

By definition, culture refers to a group or community with which we share common experiences that also shape the way we understand the world. A multicultural society exists where there is more than one culture in a society. This scenario may create tensions and bring many challenges to society as a whole. One of the challenges paused by a multicultural situation is in how one group or individual, like Malika Oufkir, with a different culture ought to respect the cultural convictions of another group without compromising its or her own cultural values. In a multicultural setting, respect for other cultures is vital to society's own survival. Malika who had a Moroccan cultural background would only survive and integrate by learning and respecting the cultural norms of the French society. But to be a multicultural person, she would have to preserve her native culture within the French society. Cultural respect is therefore one of the most crucial factors essential to the sustenance of multiculturalism.

Cultural respect is defined as the recognition, protection and continued advancement of the inherent rights, traditions, and cultures of a people. It is achieved when cultural differences are respected. It is enshrined in the role that knowledge, awareness, and behavior play in underpinning strong relationships between different groups of people. Together these three dimensions–knowledge, awareness, and behavior – should contribute to the achievement of equitable outcomes for the different cultural groups. The diversity of cultures in our world is an irreplaceable source of social and intellectual richness for all humankind. The protection and enhancement of cultural diversity should be actively promoted as an essential aspect of human development. Cultural diversity exists in time and space and demands respect for other cultures and all aspects of their belief systems. In cases where cultural values appear to be in conflict, respect for cultural diversity demands acknowledgment of the legitimacy of the cultural values of other people. Respect for diversity is the hallmark of social stability. A multicultural society comprises people of diverse backgrounds, social conditions, languages and dialects.

Respect is a central concept in maintaining social ties. Lack of respect for the customs and culture of the people around us may contribute to abuse and ill treatment. Respect for the inherent rights of people should be based on an understanding of the concept of respect which is shared by all concerned. Personal well-being depends on it and the various ways in which it must be practiced. Respect through the maintenance of good relations with various belief systems, behavioral patterns and the mores of different peoples is extremely important.

Respect for the cultural beliefs of other people is a central concept in many ethical theories (Figurski, 1310). Some theories treat it as the very essence of morality and the foundation of all other moral duties and obligations. Respect as a moral concept postulate that members of a multicultural society understand the inevitability of cultural coexistence. As people move from place to place, they carry not only their cultural beliefs with them but also the practices that come with that. This is what we saw with the case of Malika Oufkir in the introductory passage. According to Rest (1986), morality helps in the preservation and maintenance of an understanding among different groups: "Morality refers to a set of values that have to do with how humans cooperate and coordinate their activities in the service of furthering human welfare, and how they adjudicate conflict among individual interests."

Morality is an ethic. Rest (1986) distinguishes between moral behavior and moral judgment in dealing with matters of respect in cultural perspectives. The former is any course of action that services moral functions in a given situation, and moral judgment is the cognitive process by which one determines which particular behavior is morally appropriate. In a multicultural setting, moral behavior is one that acts in the interests of other groups. It is an action that will not infringe on the cultural beliefs of other people. This entails adhering to the principles of respect and goodwill.

We live in a world with dynamic social conditions with increasing awareness of social and cultural rights. In this kind of society moral judgment is essential to the peaceful coexistence of different cultures. Morality as it applies to culture has two faces, the individual as well as the social. It follows that a cultural animal, such as man, is directly influenced by his rightness or wrongness in society. At the individual level, morality demands that as a citizen an individual is obliged to respect the views of other people, which will include their cultural beliefs as well. At the social level, co-operation and shared responsibility are essential in a multicultural situation.

Moral judgment will lead to moral behavior. In his book Moral Development: Advances in Research and Theory, Rest, in addition to moral judgment, identifies three other components necessary to enhancing the practicality of cultural respect. First, individual members of a group need to be sensitive to what kind of behavior is possible in a given situation and how they would affect the interested parties. This will be followed by giving priority to behaving morally as opposed to responding with personal values that may conflict with the cultural norms of other people.

And last, when confronted with a situation in which different interests are involved, one needs the ability to follow through with the course of action that has been identified as moral.

All cultures have an inherent purpose. The purpose of any cultural group is in its goals and objectives which its members must fulfill. There is thus a chain reaction: society creates cultural groups, and these groups should act to fulfill the goals of society! Morality will ensure that different cultural groups perform in accordance with the common good of all. Cultural respect, therefore, is inevitable for society as a whole to function.

The moral response to cultural diversity is guaranteed as a form of civil rights grounded in the equality of cultures. The Vienna Declaration on human rights stipulates that in dealing with the multicultural society, "The significance of … cultural and religious backgrounds must be born in mind" (Ayton, 19). Despite this fact, however, there ought to be caution that this kind of scenario does not compromise or dilute the unquestionably universal standards of human rights. This theory is in support of the principle of cultural relativism which asserts that human values, far from being universal, vary a great deal according to different cultural perspectives. When meeting with individuals of another culture, cultural sensitivity must be balanced with values, without compromising either. To achieve this, respect for other people's cultural norms and one's values is a factor.

Effective communication is a key factor in the harmonization of cultural differences. The importance of effective communication as applied to cultural harmonization cannot be overemphasized. In discussing cultural respect as a fundamental aspect of multiculturalism, the issue of conflicts among different groups will rank high. Communicating effectively between and among groups will ensure smooth coexistence. Cultural differences need not paralyze society for fear of saying or doing the right thing. Becoming more aware of cultural differences as well as exploring similarities therein, can help interested groups communicate with each other more effectively. As Lantieri and Patti (1996) put it, "Recognizing where cultural differences are at work is the first step towards understanding and respecting each other." Cultural norms emerge as people interact. These norms in turn serve as guidelines for people's behavior and actions. For people to respect each other's cultures they need to understand the other's uniqueness. But more importantly, they need to know how to communicate effectively with each other. For the purposes of this paper, effective communication will be defined as, "The ability of two or more parties to participate fully and equally in a … conversation, each using their preferred language and/or modality, and each able to communicate in real time both expressively and receptively, clearly, and accurately…." (Lantieri and Patti, 2) In this definition two key issues emerge.

It is the issue of participating fully and equally. Where one group feels it is more superior to the other, conflicts are bound to occur. In participating fully and equally, members of each cultural group understand that they have a responsibility to the other group members. This will ensure that cultural barriers, such as disrespect for the other's manners or customs, are alleviated. Next, it is the issue of communicating expressively and receptively. For harmony to prevail in the midst of cultural differences, communicating expressively as well as receptively is essential. Where one cultural group feels it has the right to express its norms without being interrupted it should assert so. But this should be understood by the other group. This is detailed by the principles of effective communication. The sending of information or in this case, culture, must be balanced with the fact that such culture is received and understood by the other group. With regard to cultural respect, impromptu communication might be understood to be a barrier. Hence, the need for an expressive way of asserting one's cultural sentiments without undermining those of the other groups.

To illustrate the point given above, it is necessary to emphasize that the way people communicate varies widely between, and even within, cultures. Across cultures, for example, some words or phrases may be used differently. A simple "yes" may mean "may be" to one group while to another it means "definitely so." Furthermore, body language, gestures and postures may mean differently in different cultures. In one culture postures that indicate receptiveness may indicate aggressiveness in another culture.

Lee Gardenswartz and Anita Rowe compared cultural norms and values as an attempt at managing cultural diversity. This was done in lieu of the American mainstream culture compared to other cultures. The US and Canada were chosen because they were highly multicultural nations. In this comparison aspects of culture ranging from a sense of self-respect to work habits and practices were identified. The interesting results are shown in the table below.
It is plain from this table that different forms of expressions exist for similar kinds of actions or behavior in different cultural groups. Respecting and understanding these norms and values by other groups is vital for a multicultural society to thrive. For example, in an American mainstream culture explicit and direct kind of communication is preferred to implicit and indirect kind of communication in other cultures.

Cultural respect is the response to these

differences, ensuring that they do not divide a multicultural society, but rather strengthen it. Lantieri and Patti observe further, "Awareness of cultural differences doesn't have to divide us from each other…becoming more aware of our cultural differences can help us communicate with each other more effectively." Awareness of cultural differences is a fundamental factor in sustaining a multicultural society. Awareness that such differences exist for the benefit of society as a whole is an important matter. Aware that differences exist can make interested parties communicate effectively, bearing in mind the factor that cultural understanding depends on it. When this awareness is lacking, disrespect for other people's culture will be the result. Such a state of affairs could be a source of cultural tensions rather than harmony in a multicultural society.

Different cultures have different styles of communication. Learning about different ways that people communicate can enrich people's lives. These differences reflect deeper philosophies and world views which are the foundation of their culture. Understanding these deeper philosophies will broaden the picture of what the world has to offer. In this regard culture is central to what we see, how we make sense of what we see and how we express ourselves. In the words of Anthropologists Kevin Avruch and Peter Black as quoted by Lantieri and Patti (1996), "...One's own culture provides the 'lens' through which we view the world; the 'logic'... by which we order it; the 'grammar' ... by which it makes sense." Through their culture, people view the world in a particular way. What they do, how they do it and the way they think depend on their culture.

In an atmosphere of more than one culture, there are bound to be challenges. When we learn about other people's culture and begin to understand the differences, it gives us the mirror image of our own. We have the opportunity to challenge our assumptions about the right way of doing things and start to consider a variety of approaches. A chance is thus provided to learn new ways of solving problems that were not previously envisaged.

We start to understand that what makes sense to one group of people may not make sense to another at first sight. But then we realize that through communication, these differences can be used for the good of everyone which could help to unite society rather than divide it.

Sometimes cultural norms may not apply to the behavior of any particular individual. Several factors such as ethnic backgrounds, family, education, personality, and so on, can play a role in determining the way one behaves.

This is why it is arbitrary, even dangerous, to attempt to evaluate very diverse cultures by reference to a fixed value system. In their book, *Culture: A Critical Review of Concepts and Definitions*, as quoted by Passmore Kroeber and Kluckhohn, they submit, "Culture consists of patterns, explicit and implicit, of and for behavior acquired and transmitted by symbols, constituting and distinctive achievement of human groups, including their embodiments in artifacts…" Culture is a distinctive achievement of particular human groups. It is a symbolic product of group activity. The postulation here is that what has been produced by a group is much superior to an individual achievement. Hence, cultural respect follows that culture is sustained through shared symbolic experience. Emphasis should be placed on the nature of symbolically meaningful experiences.

Man as a member of society has both intrinsic and extrinsic value in what he chooses to believe in. His way of life communicated through culture plays a key role in asserting his humanity. He should be respected not only because he is a person but more so because through his culture, he contributes to the common good of all.

Man as a member of society has invested into his culture which in turn has preserved him. E.B Taylor believes that cultural respect is a prerogative man should be appraised for. He sees culture as "That complex whole which includes knowledge, belief, art, morals, laws, customs, and any other capabilities and habits acquired by man as a member of society" (Taylor, 7).

Taylor assumes that culture is wealth. One's culture is a wealth of investment which ought to be protected. This protection should be based on a clear communication of values that are contained in any culture. Members of society don't just have the duty to respect other groups' culture but also to promoting and communicating their own culture as concisely as possible. This will eliminate all misunderstandings and enhance social interaction. Effective communication is thus imperative in ensuring that the cultural norms of different groups are respected and understood in a diverse society.

The highest form of cultural expression is one becomes a multicultural person. Johan Galtung (2002) sees multiculturalism as progressing through four stages. He identifies these as intolerance, tolerance, dialogue and last, becoming a multicultural person.

He describes the intolerance stage as an antagonism stage characterized by invasion and subsequent killing of one culture by an invader.

Tolerance, on the other hand, is better than intolerance, but only a peaceful coexistence, essentially signaling that "I am so generous that I tolerate that you exist." But he contends that even this stage is not good enough in a world where different cultures will have ever broader and deeper contact.

Dialogue as a third stage is based on mutual respect and curiosity like "how wonderful that you are different from me, and then we can learn from each other and maybe develop something new."

The dialogue stage, despite being warfare with verbal means, is however, a major step forward towards becoming a multicultural person, a situation in which group members see each other as sources of mutual enrichment.

Cultural respect reaches its peak in a transition from merely multiculturalism to multicultural person. This is not simply an active coexistence of more than one culture inside one person, but also inside a society where that person is respected for what he is and in turn he has respect for the convictions of others. DuPraw and Axner identified six patterns of how cultural differences can help in understanding people who are different. They postulate that an appreciation of patterns of cultural difference can assist us in processing what it means to be different in ways that are respectful of others, not faultfinding or damaging.

In the first place, it is important to learn from generalizations about other cultures, but not to use those generalizations to stereotype or oversimplify one's ideas about another person. The best use of a generalization is to add it to one's storehouse of knowledge so that one better understands and appreciates other interesting, multi-faceted human beings. Anthropologists have discovered that the best way to really get to know another society and its culture is to live in it as an active participant rather than simply an observer. Malika's leaving Morocco and living in France typically exemplifies this idea. By physically and emotionally participating in the social interaction of society, it is possible to become accepted as a member. In practice this requires learning their language and establishing close friendship ties. It also usually involves living within the community as a member, eating what they eat, and taking part in normal family activities with them. Appreciating another culture in this way eliminates all forms of stereotypes and oversimplification of ideas about other people. In the end it results in respecting the cultural views of the other group.

It is wise not to assume that there is one right way to communicate. As a member of a multicultural society, frequently question your assumptions about the right way to communicate. For example, think about your body language; postures that indicate receptivity in one culture might indicate aggressiveness in another.

In that light regard the cultural diversity of your group and that of the other groups as distinct but mutual. Moreover, it is not appropriate to assume that breakdowns in communication occur because other people are on the wrong track. Search for ways to make communication work, rather than searching for who should receive the blame for the breakdown.

There are degrees of respect which different societies recognize. Let us consider the idea of respect in a multicultural society with a Hindu culture for example. A boy is walking in the school corridor. He gets a hard slap on his back from a senior student. One might think that this is a gesture with a bad intention, but is it? This is actually one of the most common ways of elders greeting a younger person. The senior student wouldn't give a second glance to somebody he didn't like or respect. Respect, as shown from this example, can be shown in many ways. Students call their teacher ' Sir' or 'Ma'am.' At the end of somebody's name 'ji' might be added. Among the Bemba people of Northern Zambia "ba" must be added before the name of someone older in order to express respect.

People usually expect others to treat them with respect. In the same way people should treat others with respect. A simple "excuse me" or "please move" is welcomed more than "move" or "get out of the way" when people are moving through a crowd. There are many different kinds of respect in Hindu culture. "The respect stated above should be shown to strangers" (Satyam, viii). But there are higher degrees of respect than that. If a person meets a movie star or the president of their country, they will naturally show more respect. But in the Hindu culture respect is usually gained from a person's achievements or character.

There ought to be an effort on the part of the multicultural person to listen actively and empathetically. Trying to put yourself in the other person's shoes is an empathic way of treating others with respect. Especially when another person's perceptions or ideas are very different from your own, you might need to operate at the edge of your own comfort zone. But listening actively can enable you to see as the other person sees. Usually, people who react to situations according to their preconceived ideas undermine communication. Reacting with preconceived ideas will hinder effective communication and defeat the ideals of multiculturalism.

A multicultural society, which is an antithesis of monoculturalism, advocates for a society which allows and includes distinct cultural groups to exist with equal status.

Listening attentively also involves respecting others' choices about whether to engage in communication with you.

There must be some preparation for a discussion of the past. This opportunity should be used to develop an understanding from "the other's" point of view, rather than getting defensive or impatient. Acknowledge historical events that have taken place. Parties should be open to learning more about them. Honest acknowledgment of the mistreatment and oppression that have taken place on the basis of cultural difference is vital for effective communication. This should be followed by an awareness of current power imbalances (if any) and openness to hearing each other's perceptions of those imbalances, which is also necessary for understanding each other and working together.

It is crucial to remember that cultural norms may not apply to the behavior of any particular individual. Individuals are shaped by many factors - their ethnic background, their family history, their educational levels and their personalities - which are more complicated than any cultural norm could suggest. As a member of a culturally diverse society and one who is keen at becoming a multicultural person, it is vital to gain correct interpretations if you are uncertain of what is meant by the other person before you react according to your own set of beliefs and norms.

12 | AFRICAN DIASPORA

It is not a myth that many an African sees the West, especially the US, Canada, and Europe as a paradise of hope. This is partly exacerbated by a myth that life is free from struggle in the developed nations. Many people who have not stepped a foot on the developed nations' soils somehow believe that it is a land of free dollars, carefree living, and indulgence. This attitude is mostly accelerated by the been-tos and Hollywood.

When people travel to the West for further education, for missionary activities or for a temporary visit, they return to Africa with impeccable stories. They tell of the paved and pothole-free streets, of clean and well-groomed backyards, of the free spirit of democracy and tolerance, and of a life of plenty. They report how it is so easy to find employment, and people can change jobs almost at will. They talk of the buzzing malls, of the electrified camp sites and parks, of the elevated architecture and of the unmatched technology.

Those who have not traveled also hear about the West from friends and relatives who may be there already. But most watch Hollywood movies. Everything seems calm and calculated. It is the image of life only experienced in dreams. This sends goose-bumps and a keen desire to visit or even live in the West. There is a feeling that once there, things will be so easy and free.

Despite all the flashes of a seemingly carefree living in the West, life is not as easy as it seems. While most Africans who relocate to the West find it reasonably better to live there, they are not immune from the rigor of hard work, competition and even fear of lack. Life in the West is just like anywhere else. You are rewarded for what you do. If you are hardworking and enterprising, life will be meaningful and manageable. But if you are lazy, you end up on welfare or even at the bottom of the beginning drive.

Although most governments in the West supplement people's efforts, there is no guarantee that things will just improve on their own in fact, in the capitalistic arrangement, people are subjected to a life of competition where the smartest and the luckiest survive and prosper.

The West, unlike most African governments, is blessed with developed economies. This means that people can have access to social amenities and resources. In this way, the Western life is reasonably more manageable than that in many African nations. The spirit of free competition in the West also ensures that people are rewarded for their creativity, industry, and hard work. Capitalism ensures all liberty of the ownership of property and freedom of investment. Thus, those who are keen on investing and diligence will win, and those who are lazy will lose.

The diaspora can play a vital role in the democratic and development of Africa. They can use their know-how and the expertise they have acquired to help Africa move forward. When people think about the diaspora, they usually think of those who have gone to live in the rich nations as a result of poverty in Africa. That is only partly true. There are two broad categories of people who decide to leave Africa and settle in other nations.

There are those who are privileged to own means and ways of living a life which is relatively better than a common African. Some of these people have rich and influential backgrounds in Africa. They are the sons and daughters of politicians, university professors, successful businesspersons, and members of the educated elite of the African society. These people can easily get around all the financial and legal requirements of traveling. They can easily buy air tickets and acquire easy access to visas; work permits and all the needed necessities of settling or accessing education in rich and developed countries. They can do all these because they have the means or are well known at foreign missions. Even when they are not known, they can easily influence certain officials to connect them and secure them traveling success.

The second category includes those who come from war-torn regions and countries. Some may come from areas where they are abused and denied human rights. Included in this category are those who run away from their nations for various reasons, such as political dissidents, asylum seekers, and victims of economic impoverishment. Members of this category genuinely seek refuge in the countries in which they settle. In the 1960s most of these people came from Ghana, Nigeria, South Africa, to mention but a few. In recent years, due to civil wars in most parts of Africa, most of these people are coming from just anywhere in Africa. Refugees from the Congo, Sudan, Somali, Ethiopia, and Zimbabwe may continue to flood immigration lists due to conflicts or economic hardships in these African countries.

But for whatever reason Africans find themselves in the West, they should consider it as an opportunity to help Africa. They are exposed to the best educational facilities, thriving democratic societies and freedom. They are in a position to make a clear distinction between technological advancement and lack of it. They are privileged to see firsthand the blessings of living in society that has respect for human rights and dignity. They are partakers of the fruits of economic development, and they can better understand the struggles of many an African girl or boy in the shanty compounds or villages of Africa. While many African governments are spending far too much to buy latest technologies and ideas that are making the West thrive, many Africans in the diaspora are just wasting their experiences and expertise in the malls and subways of the rich and developed nations.

African governments can do one of the two things to tap into the know-how of the diaspora. They can deliberately legislate for dual citizenships so that those in the diaspora can be empowered to move easily and help develop their nations. Dual citizenship, whenever it is allowed, is the easiest way of enabling talented and educated African immigrants to reinvest into the struggling African economies. Because a dual citizen has rights to fully participate in the governing of the two states, he or she is in the better place to share the success of one nation to the one in need. Some argue against the concept of dual citizenship for security reasons. Surely, they have a valid point. But a dual citizen is as much a citizen of one as of the other country. He or she is obliged to obey the laws of the two countries and benefit from their progress. And the fact of being a citizen of both countries enables him or her to live up to the expectations of both. This in itself is sufficient a reason why a dual citizen may protect the secrets of both nations. So far there has never been a problem in countries where dual citizenship is allowed, such as in Canada and Great Britain.

African governments should encourage free and non-conditional interactions with the diaspora. Wise governments can befit a great deal from the technical and technological know-how of those who live and work in the diaspora. The good news is that they may be able to get the same information and techno-how for free. African governments should cease from considering the Africans in the diaspora as a nuisance. They should not think of them as having arrived already. And Africans in the diaspora should not forget about Africa just because they live better and peacefully in the West. In a mutual undertaking, African governments and the diaspora should consider each other as partners in the development of Africa.

Japan and South Korea have both benefited from the Western technology. Africans who live in the West can help bring recycled technology to help develop Africa. There is nothing immoral in creatively borrowing from what has worked so well in the West and bring it to Africa. Except where intellectual or patent rights forbid, Africans in the diaspora can transmit their know-how, expertise and experiences to their brothers and sisters at home. They can volunteer to teach in schools, conduct developmental expeditions, expose young African children to civic and democratic principles, build dilapidated infrastructures and motivate confidence in the current governors. They can do all these at little or no cost to the African governments, thus saving valuable national resource and wealth for needy areas.

The problem is, do African governments have the structure to channel the diaspora's experiences into real development tools for Africa?

The sad attitude of most African governments has been viewing the diaspora as competitors rather than partners. The thinking that those who are in the Western and developed countries are somehow better off than those living in Africa is wrong.

While to some extent they may be better, only in so far as being better means having a good job and living reasonably above the poverty line, Africans can have as prosperous a life as anybody else within Africa.

In fact, most Africans who have a good paying job in Africa and are living within their means have no reason to envy their Western counterparts. Some Africans who sold all they had in Africa and settled in the developed nations come to a bitter reality that they were, after all, not very smart.

Life in Africa can be just as beautiful as life in the developed nations. But it takes knowledge to come to this truth. To some, it takes practical reality, when they finally land on the Western soil and learn that things are not easy as they thought.

13 | PUTTING IT IN CONTEXT

When Africans are discussing the historical plunder of Africa, it seems that it makes reasonable sense to distribute the blame. Thus, there are some Africans who, in fact, adduce an hypothesis that Africans have themselves contributed to the state of poverty in Africa. Then they make such allegations as poor African leadership, lack of planning, corruption, etc., have contributed to make Africa poor.

That is a misplaced thesis and should not be honored or encouraged in any discourse dealing with historical White slavery and colonialism in Africa. In fact, it is largely a colonial asphyxia camouflaged as civilized argument. Unless one has not thought about it deeply; having enslaved Africa for over 300 years, Europeans, to add salt to injury, gathered at Berlin in 1885 and decided to settle and plunder Africa in form of the Scramble for Africa. That, in essence, was adding another 150 years to the subjugation of Africa.

Then there are those, mostly European writers, who submit that Africa has failed to manage itself in the first twenty, thirty or fifty years of self-rule. This is then construed as a lack of leadership acumen in the African rants. Some racist White philosophers have gone to such inglorious postulations as to cast aspersions that Africans need to be ruled, otherwise, they can destroy everything if left by themselves.

These colonial philosophizing and argumentation lack a cogent historical context. Africa is barely sixty years "free." White Europe and America plundered the continent for over 400 years, and another close to 100 years in other forms such as neo-colonialism and corporatism. To put this in context. If Africa had plundered say Europe or America for, say, 400 years, these continents would be deserts, unproductive and impoverished banes.

That is what was done to Africa.

No leadership type is equipped to redeem such impoverishment. No amount of aid can. And no version of political engineering can, either. No Black or White leader is given such alacrity to reverse the harm White Europe and America did to Africa.

At least no meaningful reversal can be done in this present century.

There is only one option.

The 22nd Century.

By the next century, Africa would have been 150 years freed from the mental propensities of both slavery and colonialism. Africa would have totally bred a new era of economists, politicians, thinkers, and national builders. That era would not be asphyxiated on the Whiteman as a political or economic magician or savior. That generation would have been weaned from a colonial and slavery mentality. It will be a pure breed of statespersons and thinkers. It will deliver sustainable development.

Africa must be developed at whatever cost.

To begin that process, 21st Century must do the following.

First, Africans must rediscover who they were before the upheavals of slavery and colonialism. They were empire builders. They had conquered lands. They were creative and technologically savvy. And they were proud to be Black and African. They took pleasure in their culture.

Second, they must own themselves. They should not allow another race of people to own them as property or anything, less or more. They must be totally free.

Third, they must not let money and raw materials leave Africa unless it brings adequate consideration. Informed trade, and not subtle and other innuendos should define future relations between Africa and other continents.

Fourth, they must invest in Africans. African children must have access to pure African quality education, healthcare, clean water, plenty of food and a green environment. They must learn and appreciate their own heroes, languages, names, freedoms, and land before they do so for other peoples. They must care for their health. They must drink clean water and grow and eat plenty of nutritious food. Africa has all that underneath its blessed soils and azure skies. They must do as they have always done, pride in their "jungles." For it is now the jungle jingle that is the anthem of climate change and global warming combatants. Without preserving these African "jungles," there would be no green or a healthy earth tomorrow.

And fifth, they must lead the world. In 22nd Century, Africa must refuse to be a by-word, a by-stander or a buyout.

Africa shall not be a servant or a slave.

Africa must sit at the world table where global decisions are made and must not be just an *agenda* item. Africa must lead the *agenda*.

The 22nd Century should give Africa its deserved place in the affairs of the living and the community of equal nations.

ABOUT THE AUTHOR

Charles Mwewa (LLB; BA Law; BA Ed; LLM) is a prolific author and researcher, poet, novelist, lawyer, law professor and Christian apologist. Mwewa has written no less than 40 books and counting in every genre and has exhibited his works at prestigious expos like the Ottawa International Book Expo and is the winner of the Coppa Awards for his signature publication, *Zambia: Struggles of My People.*

SELECTED BOOKS BY THIS AUTHOR

1.   *ZAMBIA: Struggles of My People (First and Second Editions)*
2.   *10 FINANCIAL & WEALTH ATTITUDES TO AVOID*
3.   *10 STRATEGIES TO DEFEAT STRESS AND DEPRESSION: Creating an Internal Safeguard against Stress and Depression*
4.   *100+ REASONS TO READ BOOKS*
5.   *A CASE FOR AFRICA?S LIBERTY: The Synergistic Transformation of Africa and the West into First-World Partnerships*
6.   *A PANDEMIC POETRY, COVID-19*
7.   *ALLERGIC TO CORRUPTION: The Legacy of President Michael Sata of Zambia*
8.   *BOOK ABOUT SOMETHING: On Ultimate Purpose*
9.   *CAMPAIGN FOR AFRICA: A Provocative Crusade for the Economic and Humanitarian Decolonization of Africa*
10. *CHAMPIONS: Application of Common Sense and Biblical Motifs to Succeed in Both Worlds*
11. *CORONAVIRUS PRAYERS*
12. *HH IS THE RIGHT MAN FOR ZAMBIA: And Other Acclaimed Articles on Zambia and Africa*
13. *I BOW: 3500 Prayer Lines of Inspiration & Intercession from the Heart: Volume One*
14. *INTERUNIVERSALISM IN A NUTSHELL: For Iranian Refugee Claimants*
15. *LAW & GRACE: An Expository Study in the Rudiments of Sin and Truth*
16. *LAWS OF INFLUENCE: 7even Lessons in Transformational Leadership*

INDEX

marginalization, 96, 108

masters, 5, 33, 34, 62, 68, 89, 119, 120, 122, 137, 140

Mauritius, 16

media, 96

Mercedes Benz, 101

Mexico, 2

Microsoft, 26, 102

migrant laborers, 26

military and economic influence, 149

misinformation, 127

missionaries and explorers, 130

Mississauga, 95

Mobutu Seseko, 73

morality. *See* ethics

Morgan Tsvangirai, 77

mortgage, 79

mother-to child transmission, 55

Munyonzwe Hamalengwa, vii

Mwai Kibaki, 75

Mwewa, 71

Myles Monroe, 11

N

Namibia, 16

Nana Akufo Addo, 77

Neil van Schalkwyk. *See* vuvuzelas

Nelson Mandela, 15, 80

neo-morality, 84

Netherlands. *See* Berlin Congress

Nevers Mumba, 83

New Orleans, 150

New World (America), 128

NGO. *See* Non-Governmental Organization

Nigeria, 144, 182

Non-Governmental Organization, 9

O

OPEC, 144

open-mindedness, 4, 14

Operation Young Vote, 9

oppressive, 61, 62

Ottawa, 1

Ottawa International Book and Crafts Expo. *See* Ottawa

OYV. *See* Operation Young Vote

P

Parliament, 123

partners, 19, 29, 185, 186

patronage, 19

Paul Biya, 66

Paul Kagame. *See* Rwanda

Paulina. *See* Paulina Attitude

Pauline Attitude, 2

Pennsylvania Avenue, 134

people-centered leaders. *See* neo-morality

personal freedoms. *See* neo-

morality
self-interest, 144, 147
separation of church. *See* neo-morality
Seychelles, 16
Shakespeare, 110
shithole, 136
Sierra Leone, 16
slavery, 18, 21, 84, 86, 104, 112, 121, 122, 123, 125, 127, 131, 133, 136, 137
social competency. *See* inferior race
socialism. *See* communism
Somali, 182
South Africa, 16, 35, 80, 101, 103, 122, 132, 145, 182
sovereignty, 7, 85, 108
Spain. *See* Berlin Congress
special interests. *See* lobbyists
standard of living, 42, 93
stigmatization, 54
Struggles of My People, 115, 116, 135, 193, 195
succession, 12, 13, 73, 74
Sudan, 34, 75, 81, 103, 150, 182
sustainable, 10, 12, 29, 44, 91, 121, 154
Sweden-Norway. *See* Berlin Congress

T

T.H Green, 93

technocrats, 27
technology, 36, 43, 50, 82, 83, 104, 108, 115, 132, 145, 148, 179, 185
Teodoro Obiang Nguema Mbasogo, 16, 66
terra nullius, 19, 130
terrorism, 147
the West, 195
Toronto, 116
trade, 19, 26, 34, 46, 47, 86, 119, 122, 123, 136, 145, 148
Trans-Atlantic Slave Trade. *See* Trans-Atlantic Slavery
Trans-Atlantic Slavery, 117, 118, 119
treason, 116
tribalism, 3
Tsunami, 150
Turkey. *See* Berlin Congress

U

Ukraine, 40, 61, 84, 144, 150
underdevelopment, 17
unemployment. *See* neo-morality
unemployment insurance, 93
unique, 105, 106, 112, 144, 145
United Airlines, 49
United Kingdom. *See* Security Council
United Nations, 145

www.ingramcontent.com/pod-product-compliance
Lightning Source LLC
Chambersburg PA
CBHW050114280326
41933CB00010B/1100